PRESENTED TO:

_____

FROM:

_____

DATE:

_____

# PROTECTION!

## finding safety in an unsafe world

**FOR WOMEN**

*The quoted ideas expressed in this book (but not Scripture verses) are not, in all cases, exact quotations, as some have been edited for clarity and brevity. In all cases, the author has attempted to maintain the speaker's original intent. In some cases, quoted material for this book was obtained from secondary sources, primarily print media. While every effort was made to ensure the accuracy of these sources, the accuracy cannot be guaranteed. For additions, deletions, corrections, or clarifications in future editions of this text, please write Freeman-Smith.*

Scripture quotations are taken from:

The Holy Bible, King James Version (KJV)

The Holy Bible, New International Version (NIV) Copyright © 1973, 1978, 1984, by International Bible Society. Used by permission of Zondervan Publishing House. All rights reserved.

The Holy Bible, New King James Version (NKJV) Copyright © 1982 by Thomas Nelson, Inc. Used by permission.

Holy Bible, New Living Translation, (NLT) copyright © 1996. Used by permission of Tyndale House Publishers, Inc., Wheaton, Illinois 60189. All rights reserved.

The Message (MSG)- This edition issued by contractual arrangement with NavPress, a division of The Navigators, U.S.A. Originally published by NavPress in English as THE MESSAGE: The Bible in Contemporary Language copyright 2002-2003 by Eugene Peterson. All rights reserved.

New Century Version®. (NCV) Copyright © 1987, 1988, 1991 by Word Publishing, a division of Thomas Nelson, Inc. All rights reserved. Used by permission.

The New American Standard Bible®, (NASB) Copyright © 1960, 1962, 1963, 1968, 1971, 1972, 1973, 1975, 1977, 1995 by The Lockman Foundation. Used by permission.

The Holman Christian Standard Bible™ (HCSB) Copyright © 1999, 2000, 2001 by Holman Bible Publishers. Used by permission.

Cover Design by Kim Russell / Wahoo Designs
Page Layout by Bart Dawson

ISBN 978-1-60587-348-0

*Printed in the United States of America*

# PROTECTION!
### finding
### safety
### in an
### unsafe
### world

FOR WOMEN

# INTRODUCTION

This world can be a dangerous place, a place of trials, temptations, and troubles. Life would be easier (easier, but not better) if your faith were never challenged—if you never experienced doubts, or temptations, or worries, or frustrations. But it doesn't work that way. Hundreds of times each day, your faith is challenged as God provides you with opportunities to do the right thing by overcoming a negative emotion, or by extending a helping hand, or by speaking an encouraging word, or by doing a thousand other seemingly insignificant tasks that make your world a kinder, gentler, happier place. When these opportunities occur, you have a choice: you can either accept God's challenge and follow His path, or you can ignore His calling and live with the consequences. The ideas in this book will encourage you to do the right thing by following God's lead and by putting your faith to work.

To God, there are no insignificant acts of kindness. For Him, there are no small favors, no unimportant good deeds, no minor acts of mercy, and no inconsequential acts of obedience. To God, everything you do has major implications within His kingdom. He takes your actions seriously, and so should you.

This book contains devotional readings that are intended to remind you that God's provision is the ultimate security. The text is divided into 30 chapters, one for each day of the month. Each chapter contains Bible verses, quotations, brief essays, and timely tips, all of which can help you focus your thoughts on the countless blessings and opportunities that God has placed before you.

During the next 30 days, please try this experiment: read one chapter each morning. If you're a woman who is already committed to a daily worship time, this book will enrich that experience. If you are not, the simple act of giving God a few minutes each morning will change the tone and direction of your life.

Your daily devotional time can be habit-forming, and should be. The first few minutes of each day are invaluable. So treat them that way, and offer them to God.

## DAY 1

# FINDING A SAFE PLACE
# IN AN UNSAFE WORLD

*Finally, be strong in the Lord and
in his mighty power. Put on the full armor of God
so that you can take your stand
against the devil's schemes.*

—

EPHESIANS 6:10-11 NIV

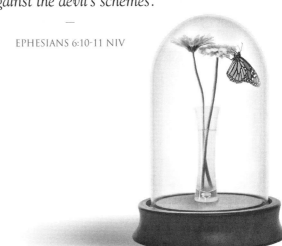

The Lord God of heaven and earth, the Almighty
Creator of all things, He who holds the universe in
His hand as though it were a very little thing, He is your
Shepherd, and He has charged Himself with the care
and keeping of you, as a shepherd is charged
with the care and keeping of his sheep.

—

HANNAH WHITALL SMITH

These are dangerous times, times when temptations, distractions, and dangers can be encountered in more ways, and in more places, than ever before.

We live in this dangerous world, but we should not worship it—yet at every turn, or so it seems, we are tempted to do otherwise. As Warren Wiersbe correctly observed, "Because the world is deceptive, it is dangerous."

The world seems to cry, "Worship me with your time, your money, your energy, your thoughts, and your life!" But if we are wise, we won't fall prey to that temptation.

If you wish to find genuine security, and build a better life in the process, you must distance yourself from the enticements and diversions of modern-day society. But distancing yourself isn't easy, especially when so many societal forces are struggling to capture your attention, your participation, and your money.

C. S. Lewis said, "Aim at heaven and you will get earth thrown in; aim at earth and you will get neither." That's good advice. You're likely to hit what you aim at, so aim high . . . aim at heaven. When you do, you'll discover the genuine security that God offers to believers (like you) who honor God by obeying His commandments.

## SLOW DOWN AND THINK

Are you sometimes just a little too impulsive? Do you occasionally leap before you look? If so, you may find it helpful (and ultimately comforting) to take a careful look at what the Bible says about impulsiveness.

Proverbs 22:3 offers this warning: "A prudent person foresees the danger ahead and takes precautions; the simpleton goes blindly on and suffers the consequences" (NLT). And, Proverbs 19:2 teaches: "Enthusiasm without knowledge is not good. If you act too quickly, you might make a mistake" (NCV). So, the Bible teaches us to be cautious, but the world often tempts us to behave otherwise. Sometimes, we're faced with powerful temptations to be impetuous, reckless, and undisciplined. These are temptations we must resist.

When you make a habit of thinking first and acting second, you'll be comforted in the knowledge that you're

incorporating God's wisdom into the fabric of your life. And, you'll earn the rewards that the Creator inevitably bestows upon those who take the time to look—and to think—before they leap.

A mighty fortress is our God, a bulwark never failing
Our helper He, amid the flood of mortal ills prevailing
For still our ancient foe doth seek to work us woe
His craft and power are great, armed with cruel hate,
Our earth is not his equal.

—

MARTIN LUTHER

## MORE FROM GOD'S WORD ABOUT FINDING SAFETY IN GOD'S PROMISES

*The Lord says, "I will make you wise and show you where to go. I will guide you and watch over you."*

PSALM 32:8 NCV

*For the eyes of the Lord range throughout the earth to strengthen those whose hearts are fully committed to him.*

2 CHRONICLES 16:9 NIV

*Be strong and courageous, and do the work. Do not be afraid or discouraged, for the Lord God, my God, is with you.*

1 CHRONICLES 28:20 NIV

*Let us hold fast the confession of our hope without wavering, for He who promised is faithful.*

HEBREWS 10:23 NASB

*The Lord is my rock, my fortress, and my deliverer, my God, my mountain where I seek refuge. My shield, the horn of my salvation, my stronghold, my refuge, and my Savior.*

2 SAMUEL 22:2-3 HCSB

## MORE POWERFUL IDEAS ABOUT THE
## ULTIMATE SOURCE OF SECURITY: GOD

He goes before us, follows behind us, and hems us safe inside the realm of His protection.

BETH MOORE

It is an act of the will to allow God to be our refuge. Otherwise we live outside of his love and protection, wondering why we feel alone and afraid.

MARY MORRISON SUGGS

Being loved by Him whose opinion matters most gives us the security to risk loving, too—even loving ourselves.

GLORIA GAITHER

### A TIP FOR TODAY

Remember: life is God's gift to you— taking good care of yourself is your gift to God.

We are never out of reach of Satan's devices, so we must never be without the whole armor of God.

WARREN WIERSBE

## A PRAYER FOR TODAY

*Lord, You have promised that You will provide for my needs, and I trust that promise. But sometimes, because of my imperfect faith, I fall prey to worry and doubt. Today, give me the courage to trust You completely. You are my protector, Dear Lord; let me praise You, let me love You, and let me trust in the perfect wisdom of Your plan. Amen*

## TODAY'S THOUGHTS

My thoughts about God's willingness to lead me and protect me.

_____

_____

_____

_____

_____

_____

_____

_____

15

DAY 2

# GOD'S PROTECTION

*Though I sit in darkness, the Lord will be my light.*

MICAH 7:8 HCSB

God will never let you sink under your circumstances.
He always provides a safety net and
His love always encircles.

—

BARBARA JOHNSON

Have you ever faced challenges that seemed too big to handle? Have you ever faced big problems that, despite your best efforts, simply could not be solved? If so, you know how uncomfortable it is to feel helpless in the face of difficult circumstances. Thankfully, even when there's nowhere else to turn, you can turn your thoughts and prayers to God, and He will respond.

God's hand uplifts those who turn their hearts and prayers to Him. Count yourself among that number. When you do, you can live courageously and joyfully, knowing that "this too will pass"—but that God's love for you will not. And you can draw strength from the knowledge that you are a marvelous creation, loved, protected, and up-lifted by the ever-present hand of God.

## OPEN YOUR HEART TO HIM

St. Augustine observed, "God loves each of us as if there were only one of us." Do you believe those words? Do you

seek to have an intimate, one-on-one relationship with your Heavenly Father, or are you satisfied to keep Him at a "safe" distance?

Sometimes, in the crush of our daily duties, God may seem far away, but He is not. God is everywhere we have ever been and everywhere we will ever go. He is with us night and day; He knows our thoughts and our prayers. And, when we earnestly seek Him, we will find Him because He is here, waiting patiently for us to reach out to Him.

Today, as you carve out quiet moments of thanksgiving and praise for your Heavenly Father, open yourself to His presence and to His love. He is here, waiting. His love is here, always. Accept it—now—and be blessed.

Things can be very difficult for us,
but nothing is too hard for Him.

—

CHARLES STANLEY

## MORE FROM GOD'S WORD ABOUT
## HIS PROTECTION

*The Lord is my strength and song, and He has become my salvation; He is my God, and I will praise Him.*

EXODUS 15:2 NKJV

*The Lord your God in your midst, The Mighty One, will save; He will rejoice over you with gladness, He will quiet you with His love, He will rejoice over you with singing.*

ZEPHANIAH 3:17 NKJV

*God is my shield, saving those whose hearts are true and right.*

PSALM 7:10 NLT

*Those who trust the Lord are like Mount Zion, which sits unmoved forever. As the mountains surround Jerusalem, the Lord surrounds his people now and forever.*

PSALM 125:1-2 NCV

*But the Lord will be a refuge for His people.*

JOEL 3:16 HCSB

## MORE POWERFUL IDEAS ABOUT
## GOD'S PROTECTION

We all go through pain and sorrow, but the presence of God, like a warm, comforting blanket, can shield us and protect us, and allow the deep inner joy to surface, even in the most devastating circumstances.

BARBARA JOHNSON

God helps those who help themselves, but there are times when we are quite incapable of helping ourselves. That's when God stoops down and gathers us in His arms like a mother lifts a sick child, and does for us what we cannot do for ourselves.

RUTH BELL GRAHAM

### A TIP FOR TODAY

Through good times and bad, God is always with you, and you are always protected.

God will not permit any troubles to come upon us unless He has a specific plan by which great blessing can come out of the difficulty.

PETER MARSHALL

## A PRAYER FOR TODAY

*Lord, sometimes life is difficult. Sometimes, I am worried, weary, or heartbroken. And sometimes, I encounter powerful temptations to disobey Your commandments. But, when I lift my eyes to You, Father, You strengthen me. When I am weak, You lift me up. Today, I will turn to You for strength, for hope, for direction, and for deliverance. Amen*

## TODAY'S THOUGHTS

My thoughts about God's power and His love.

## DAY 3

# MAKING WISE CHOICES
# AND SAFE CHOICES

*I am offering you life or death, blessings or curses.*
*Now, choose life! . . .*
*To choose life is to love the Lord your God,*
*obey him, and stay close to him.*

—

DEUTERONOMY 30:19-20 NCV

Choices can change our lives profoundly.
The choice to mend a broken relationship, to say "yes"
to a difficult assignment, to lay aside some important
work to play with a child, to visit some
forgotten person—these small choices may
affect many lives eternally.

—

GLORIA GAITHER

L ife is a series of choices. From the instant we wake in the morning until the moment we nod off to sleep at night, we make countless decisions: decisions about the things we do, decisions about the words we speak, and decisions about the thoughts we choose to think. Simply put, the quality of those decisions determines the quality of our lives.

As believers who have been saved by a loving and merciful God, we have every reason to make wise choices and safe choices. Yet sometimes, amid the inevitable hustle and bustle of life here on earth, we allow ourselves to behave in ways that we know are displeasing to our Creator. When we do, we forfeit the joy and the peace that we might otherwise experience through Him.

As you consider the next step in your life's journey, take time to consider how many things in this life you can control: your thoughts, your words, your priorities, and

your actions, for starters. And then, if you sincerely want to discover God's purpose for your life, make choices that are pleasing to Him. He deserves no less . . . and neither do you.

Sometimes, because you're an imperfect human being, you may become so wrapped up in meeting society's expectations that you fail to focus on God's expectations. To do so is a mistake of major proportions—don't make it. Instead, seek God's guidance as you focus your energies on becoming the best "you" that you can possibly be. And, when it comes to matters of conscience, seek approval not from your peers, but from your Creator.

Whom will you try to please today: God or man? Your primary obligation is not to please imperfect men and women. Your obligation is to strive diligently to meet the expectations of an all-knowing and perfect God. Trust Him always. Love Him always. Praise Him always. And make choices that please Him. Always.

## MORE FROM GOD'S WORD ABOUT
## WISE CHOICES

*So I strive always to keep my conscience clear before God and man.*

ACTS 24:16 NIV

*The thing you should want most is God's kingdom and doing what God wants. Then all these other things you need will be given to you.*

MATTHEW 6:33 NCV

*If you don't know what you're doing, pray to the Father. He loves to help. You'll get his help, and won't be condescended to when you ask for it. Ask boldly, believingly, without a second thought. People who "worry their prayers" are like wind-whipped waves. Don't think you're going to get anything from the Master that way, adrift at sea, keeping all your options open.*

JAMES 1:5-8 MSG

*Above all and before all, do this: Get Wisdom! Write this at the top of your list: Get Understanding!*

PROVERBS 4:7 MSG

## MORE POWERFUL IDEAS ABOUT
## MAKING WISE DECISIONS

Faith is not a feeling; it is action. It is a willed choice.

ELISABETH ELLIOT

The Reference Point for the Christian is the Bible. All values, judgments, and attitudes must be gauged in relationship to this Reference Point.

RUTH BELL GRAHAM

Live your lives in love, the same sort of love which Christ gives us, and which He perfectly expressed when He gave Himself as a sacrifice to God.

CORRIE TEN BOOM

### A TIP FOR TODAY

Every step of your life's journey is a choice . . . and the quality of those choices determines the quality of the journey.

Life is a series of choices between the bad, the good, and the best. Everything depends on how we choose.

VANCE HAVNER

## A PRAYER FOR TODAY

*Heavenly Father, I have many choices to make. Help me choose wisely as I follow in the footsteps of Your only begotten Son. Amen*

## TODAY'S THOUGHTS

My thoughts about the rewards of making wise choices today and every day.

_____

_____

_____

_____

_____

_____

_____

_____

_____

_____

DAY 4

# BEWARE OF THE ENEMY

*Therefore, submit to God. But resist the Devil,*
*and he will flee from you. Draw near to God,*
*and He will draw near to you.*
*Cleanse your hands, sinners, and purify*
*your hearts, double-minded people!*

—

JAMES 4:7-8 HCSB

We are in a continual battle with the spiritual forces
of evil, but we will triumph when we yield
to God's leading and call on His powerful
presence in prayer.

—

SHIRLEY DOBSON

This world is God's creation, and it contains the wonderful fruits of His handiwork. But, the world also contains countless opportunities to stray from God's will. Temptations are everywhere, and the devil, it seems, never takes a day off. Our task, as believers, is to turn away from temptation and to place our lives squarely in the center of God's will.

In his letter to Jewish Christians, Peter offered a stern warning: "Your adversary, the devil, prowls around like a roaring lion, seeking someone to devour" (1 Peter 5:8 NASB). What was true in New Testament times is equally true in our own. Evil is indeed abroad in the world, and Satan continues to sow the seeds of destruction far and wide. In a very real sense, our world is at war: good versus evil, sin versus righteousness, hope versus suffering, praise versus apathy. As Christians, we must ensure that we place ourselves squarely on the right side of these conflicts: God's side. How can we do it? By thoughtfully studying God's Word, by regularly worshiping with fellow believers,

and by guarding our hearts and minds against the subtle temptations of the enemy. When we do, we are protected.

Are you a woman who is determined to stand up against evil whenever and wherever you confront it? And are you fully prepared to distance yourself from the countless temptations that have become so thoroughly woven into the fabric of society? If so, congratulations. That means you're an active-duty participant in the battle against a powerful and dangerous adversary. And with God's help, you're destined to win the battle and the war.

Light is stronger than darkness—
darkness cannot "comprehend" or "overcome" it.

—

ANNE GRAHAM LOTZ

## MORE FROM GOD'S WORD ABOUT EVIL

*Do not be conquered by evil, but conquer evil with good.*

ROMANS 12:21 HCSB

*For everyone who practices wicked things hates the light and avoids it, so that his deeds may not be exposed. But anyone who lives by the truth comes to the light, so that his works may be shown to be accomplished by God.*

JOHN 3:20-21 HCSB

*He replied, "Every plant that My heavenly Father didn't plant will be uprooted."*

MATTHEW 15:13 HCSB

*But the path of the just is like the shining sun, that shines ever brighter unto the perfect day. The way of the wicked is like darkness; they do not know what makes them stumble.*

PROVERBS 4:18-19 NKJV

*Don't consider yourself to be wise; fear the Lord and turn away from evil.*

PROVERBS 3:7 HCSB

## MORE POWERFUL IDEAS ABOUT
## THE DANGERS OF EVIL

Where God's ministers are most successful, there the powers of darkness marshal their forces for the conflict.

LOTTIE MOON

Christianity isn't a religion about going to Sunday school, potluck suppers, being nice, holding car washes, sending your secondhand clothes off to Mexico—as good as those things might be. This is a world at war.

JOHN ELDREDGE

The descent to hell is easy, and those who begin by worshipping power soon worship evil.

C. S. LEWIS

### A TIP FOR TODAY

Your world is full of distractions and temptations. Your challenge is to live in the world but not be of the world.

Holiness has never been the driving force of the majority. It is, however, mandatory for anyone who wants to enter the kingdom.

ELISABETH ELLIOT

## A PRAYER FOR TODAY

*Lord, strengthen my walk with You. Evil comes in many disguises, and sometimes it is only with Your help that I can recognize right from wrong. Your presence in my life enables me to choose truth and to live a life pleasing to You. May I always live in Your presence. Amen*

## TODAY'S THOUGHTS

My thoughts about the dangerous temptations that face me and my loved ones.

# FINDING A SAFE PLACE
# BY DISCOVERING
# GOD'S PEACE

*Finally, brethren, whatever things are true,*
*whatever things are noble, whatever things are just,*
*whatever things are pure, whatever things are lovely,*
*whatever things are of good report,*
*if there is any virtue and if there is*
*anything praiseworthy—meditate*
*on these things.*

PHILIPPIANS 4:7-8 NKJV

The fruit of our placing all things in God's hands is
the presence of His abiding peace in our hearts.

—

HANNAH WHITALL SMITH

Have you found the lasting peace that can—and should—be yours through Jesus Christ? Or are you still chasing the illusion of "peace and happiness" that the world promises but cannot deliver?

The beautiful words of John 14:27 promise that Jesus offers peace, not as the world gives, but as He alone gives: "Peace I leave with you. My peace I give to you. I do not give to you as the world gives. Your heart must not be troubled or fearful" (HCSB). Your challenge is to accept Christ's peace into your heart and then, as best you can, to share His peace with your neighbors. But sometimes, that's easier said than done.

If you are a person with lots of obligations and plenty of responsibilities, it is simply a fact of life: you worry. From time to time, you worry about finances, safety, health, home, family, or about countless other concerns, some great and some small. Where is the best place to take your worries? Take them to God . . . and leave them there.

The Scottish preacher George McDonald observed,  "It has been well said that no man ever sank under the burden of the day. It is when tomorrow's burden is added to the burden of today that the weight is more than a man can bear. Never load yourselves so, my friends. If you find yourselves so loaded, at least remember this: it is your own doing, not God's. He begs you to leave the future to Him."

Today, as a gift to yourself, to your family, and to your friends, claim the inner peace that is your spiritual birthright: the peace of Jesus Christ. Christ is standing at the door, waiting patiently for you to invite Him to reign over your heart. His eternal peace is offered freely. Claim it today.

## TIME FOR SILENCE

The world seems to grow louder day by day, and our senses seem to be invaded at every turn. But, if we allow the distractions of a clamorous society to separate us from God's peace, we do ourselves a profound disservice. Our task, as dutiful believers, is to carve out moments of silence in a world filled with noise.

If we are to maintain righteous minds and compassionate hearts, we must take time each day for prayer and for meditation. We must make ourselves still in the presence of our Creator. We must quiet our minds and our hearts so that we might sense God's will and His love.

Has the busy pace of life robbed you of the peace that God has promised? If so, it's time to reorder your priorities and your life. Nothing is more important than the time you spend with your Heavenly Father. So be still and claim the inner peace that is found in the silent moments you spend with God. His peace is offered freely; it has been paid for in full; it is yours for the asking. So ask. And then share.

In the center of a hurricane there is absolute quiet
and peace. There is no safer place than
in the center of the will of God.

—

CORRIE TEN BOOM

## MORE FROM GOD'S WORD ABOUT PEACE

*If possible, on your part, live at peace with everyone.*

ROMANS 12:18 HCSB

*Abundant peace belongs to those who love Your instruction; nothing makes them stumble.*

PSALM 119:165 HCSB

*Blessed are the peacemakers, for they shall be called sons of God.*

MATTHEW 5:9 NKJV

*And suddenly there was with the angel a multitude of the heavenly host praising God and saying: "Glory to God in the highest, and on earth peace, goodwill toward men!"*

LUKE 2:13-14 NKJV

*So then, we must pursue what promotes peace and what builds up one another.*

ROMANS 14:19 HCSB

## MORE POWERFUL IDEAS ABOUT
## FINDING PEACE

I believe that in every time and place it is within our power to acquiesce in the will of God—and what peace it brings to do so!

ELISABETH ELLIOT

When we do what is right, we have contentment, peace, and happiness.

BEVERLY LAHAYE

Prayer guards hearts and minds and causes God to bring peace out of chaos.

BETH MOORE

To know God as He really is—in His essential nature and character—is to arrive at a citadel of peace that circumstances may storm, but can never capture.

CATHERINE MARSHALL

### A TIP FOR TODAY

Jesus was busy, but peaceful. When you follow Him, you, too, can be both busy and peaceful.

## A PRAYER FOR TODAY

*Dear Lord, when I turn my thoughts and prayers to You, I feel the peace that You intend for my life. But sometimes, Lord, I distance myself from You; sometimes, I am distracted by the busyness of the day or the demands of the moment. When I am worried or anxious, Father, turn my thoughts back to You. You are the Giver of all things good, and You give me peace when I draw close to You. Help me to trust Your will, to follow Your commands, and to accept Your peace, today and forever. Amen*

## TODAY'S THOUGHTS

My thoughts about what it means to experience "the peace which surpasses all understanding."

## DAY 6

# MANAGING STRESS

*The peace of God, which surpasses
all understanding, will guard your hearts
and minds through Christ Jesus.*

—

PHILIPPIANS 4:7 NKJV

Don't be overwhelmed.
Take it one day and one prayer at a time.

—

STORMIE OMARTIAN

Stressful days are an inevitable fact of modern life. And how do we best cope with the challenges of our demanding, 21st-century world? By turning our days and our lives over to God. Elisabeth Elliot writes, "If my life is surrendered to God, all is well. Let me not grab it back, as though it were in peril in His hand but would be safer in mine!" Yet even the most devout Christian woman may, at times, seek to grab the reins of her life and proclaim, "I'm in charge!" To do so is foolish, prideful, and stressful.

When we seek to impose our own wills upon the world—or upon other people—we invite stress into our lives . . . needlessly. But, when we turn our lives and our hearts over to God—when we accept His will instead of seeking vainly to impose our own—we discover the inner peace that can be ours through Him.

Do you feel overwhelmed by the stresses of daily life? Turn your concerns and your prayers over to God. Trust Him. Trust Him completely. Trust Him today. Trust Him always. When it comes to the inevitable challenges of this day, hand them over to God completely and without reser-

vation. He knows your needs and will meet those needs in His own way and in His own time if you let Him.

## SLOWING DOWN THE MERRY-GO-ROUND

Every major change, whether bad or good, puts stress on you and your family. That's why it's sensible to plan things so that you don't invite too many changes into your life at once. Of course, you'll be tempted to do otherwise. Once you land that new job, you'll be sorely tempted to buy the new house and the new car. Or if you've just gotten married, you'll be tempted to buy everything in sight— while the credit card payments mount. Don't do it!

When it comes to making big changes or big purchases, proceed slowly. Otherwise, you may find yourself uncomfortably perched atop a merry-go-round that is much easier to start than it is to stop.

*God, who comforts the downcast, comforted us. . . .*

2 CORINTHIANS 7:6 NIV

## MORE FROM GOD'S WORD ABOUT
## OVERCOMING ADVERSITY

*LORD, help! they cried in their trouble, and he saved them from their distress.*

PSALM 107:13 NLT

*You have allowed me to suffer much hardship, but you will restore me to life again and lift me up from the depths of the earth. You will restore me to even greater honor and comfort me once again.*

PSALM 71:20-21 NLT

*When my heart is overwhelmed: lead me to the rock that is higher than I.*

PSALM 61:2 KJV

*Trust God from the bottom of your heart; don't try to figure out everything on your own. Listen for God's voice in everything you do, everywhere you go; he's the one who will keep you on track.*

PROVERBS 3:5-6 MSG

## MORE POWERFUL IDEAS ABOUT MANAGING STRESS

The better acquainted you become with God, the less tensions you feel and the more peace you possess.

CHARLES ALLEN

Satan does some of his worst work on exhausted Christians when nerves are frayed and the mind is faint.

VANCE HAVNER

A divine strength is given to those who yield themselves to the Father and obey what He tells them to do.

WARREN WIERSBE

The happiest people I know are the ones who have learned how to hold everything loosely and have given the worrisome, stress-filled, fearful details of their lives into God's keeping.

CHARLES SWINDOLL

### A TIP FOR TODAY

Prayer is a powerful tool for managing stress, so pray often and early.

## A PRAYER FOR TODAY

*Dear Lord, sometimes the stresses of the day leave me tired and frustrated. Renew my energy, Father, and give me perspective and peace. Let me draw comfort and courage from Your promises, from Your love, and from Your Son. Amen*

## TODAY'S THOUGHTS

My thoughts about some common-sense ways that I can manage stress.

_____

_____

_____

_____

_____

_____

_____

_____

_____

## DAY 7

# ASK HIM

*So I say to you, keep asking,*
*and it will be given to you.*
*Keep searching, and you will find.*
*Keep knocking, and the door will be opened to you.*

———

LUKE 11:9 HCSB

God will help us become the people we are meant to be,
if only we will ask Him.

—

HANNAH WHITALL SMITH

How often do you ask God for His help and His wisdom? Occasionally? Intermittently? Whenever you experience a crisis? Hopefully not. Hopefully, you've acquired the habit of asking for God's assistance early and often. And hopefully, you have learned to seek His guidance in every aspect of your life.

Jesus made it clear to His disciples: they should petition God to meet their needs. So should you. Genuine, heartfelt prayer produces powerful changes in you and in your world. When you lift your heart to God, you open yourself to a never-ending source of divine wisdom and infinite love.

James 5:16 makes a promise that God intends to keep: when you pray earnestly, fervently, and often, great things will happen. Too many people, however, are too timid or too pessimistic to ask God to do big things. Please don't count yourself among their number.

God can do great things through you if you have the courage to ask Him (and the determination to keep asking Him). But don't expect Him to do all the work. When you do your part, He will do His part—and when He does, you can expect miracles to happen.

The Bible promises that God will guide you if you let Him. Your job is to let Him. But sometimes, you will be tempted to do otherwise. Sometimes, you'll be tempted to go along with the crowd; other times, you'll be tempted to do things your way, not God's way. When you feel those temptations, resist them.

God has promised that when you ask for His help, He will not withhold it. So ask. Ask Him to meet the needs of your day. Ask Him to lead you, to protect you, and to correct you. Then, trust the answers He gives.

God stands at the door and waits. When you knock, He opens. When you ask, He answers. Your task, of course, is to make God a full partner in every aspect of your life—in good times and in hard times—and to seek His guidance prayerfully, confidently, and often.

*If you need wisdom—if you want to know what*
*God wants you to do—ask him, and he will gladly tell you.*
*He will not resent your asking.*

—

JAMES 1:5 NLT

49

## MORE FROM GOD'S WORD ABOUT ASKING
## HIM FOR THE THINGS YOU NEED

*From now on, whatever you request along the lines of who I am and what I am doing, I'll do it. That's how the Father will be seen for who he is in the Son. I mean it. Whatever you request in this way, I'll do.*

JOHN 14:13-14 MSG

*You did not choose me, but I chose you and appointed you to go and bear fruit—fruit that will last. Then the Father will give you whatever you ask in my name.*

JOHN 15:16 NIV

*Until now you have not asked for anything in my name. Ask and you will receive, so that your joy will be the fullest possible joy.*

JOHN 16:24 NCV

*You fathers—if your children ask for a fish, do you give them a snake instead? Or if they ask for an egg, do you give them a scorpion? Of course not! If you sinful people know how to give good gifts to your children, how much more will your heavenly Father give the Holy Spirit to those who ask him.*

LUKE 11:11-13 NLT

## MORE POWERFUL IDEAS ABOUT ASKING GOD

By asking in Jesus' name, we're making a request not only in His authority, but also for His interests and His benefit.

SHIRLEY DOBSON

The God of the galaxies is the God who knows when your heart is broken—and He can heal it!

WARREN WIERSBE

All we have to do is to acknowledge our need, move from self-sufficiency to dependence, and ask God to become our hiding place.

BILL HYBELS

Don't be afraid to ask your heavenly Father for anything you need. Indeed, nothing is too small for God's attention or too great for his power.

DENNIS SWANBERG

### A TIP FOR TODAY

When you ask God for His assistance, He hears your request— and in His own time, He answers. If you need more, ask more.

## A PRAYER FOR TODAY

*Dear Lord, when I have questions or fears, I will turn to You. When I am weak, I will seek Your strength. When I am discouraged, Father, I will be mindful of Your love and Your grace. I will ask You for the things I need, Father, and I will trust Your answers, today and forever. Amen*

## TODAY'S THOUGHTS

My thoughts about the wisdom of asking God for the things I need.

_____

_____

_____

_____

_____

_____

_____

_____

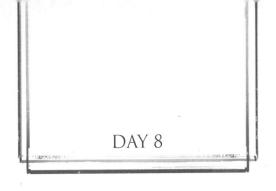

DAY 8

# MAKING PEACE
# WITH THE PAST

*Peace I leave with you, my peace I give unto you:*
*not as the world giveth, give I unto you.*
*Let not your heart be troubled,*
*neither let it be afraid.*

JOHN 14:27 KJV

If you are God's child, you are no longer bound
to your past or to what you were.
You are a brand new creature in Christ Jesus.

—

KAY ARTHUR

Some of life's greatest roadblocks are not the ones we see through the windshield; they are, instead, the roadblocks that seem to fill the rearview mirror. Because we are imperfect human beings who lack perfect control over our thoughts, we may allow ourselves to become "stuck" in the past—even though we know better. Instead of focusing our thoughts and energies on the opportunities of today, we may allow painful memories to fill our minds and sap our strength. We simply can't seem to let go of our pain, so we relive it again and again . . . with predictably unfortunate consequences. Thankfully, God has other plans.

Philippians 3:13-14 instructs us to focus on the future, not the past: "One thing I do, forgetting those things which are behind and reaching forward to those things which are ahead, I press toward the goal for the prize of the upward call of God in Christ Jesus" (NKJV). Yet for many of us, focusing on the future is difficult indeed. Why? Part of the problem has to do with forgiveness. When we find ourselves focusing too intently on the past, it's a sure sign

that we need to focus, instead, on a more urgent need: the need to forgive. Focusing too intently on the past is, almost without exception, futile. No amount of anger or bitterness can change what happened yesterday. Tears can't change the past; regrets can't change it. Our worries won't change the past, and neither will our complaints. Simply put, the past is, and always will be, the past. Forever.

Can you summon both the courage and the wisdom to accept your past and move on with your life? Can you accept the reality that yesterday—and all the yesterdays before it—are gone? And, can you entrust all those yesterdays to God? Hopefully you can.

Once you have made peace with your past, you are free to become fully engaged in the present. And when you become fully engaged in the present, you are then free to build a better future for yourself and your loved ones.

If you've endured a difficult past, learn from it, but don't live in it. Instead, build your future on a firm foundation of trust and forgiveness: trust in your Heavenly Father, and forgiveness for all His children, including yourself. Give all your yesterdays to God, and celebrate this day with hope in your heart and praise on your lips. Your Creator intends to use you in wonderful, unexpected ways if you let Him. But first, God wants you to make peace with your past . . . and He wants you to do it now.

# MORE FROM GOD'S WORD ABOUT THE PAST

*Do not remember the past events, pay no attention to things of old. Look, I am about to do something new; even now it is coming. Do you not see it? Indeed, I will make a way in the wilderness, rivers in the desert.*

ISAIAH 43:18-19 HCSB

*I do not consider myself yet to have taken hold of it. But one thing I do: Forgetting what is behind and straining toward what is ahead, I press on toward the goal to win the prize for which God has called me heavenward in Christ Jesus.*

PHILIPPIANS 3:13-14 NIV

*Create in me a pure heart, O God, and renew a steadfast spirit within me.*

PSALM 51:10 NIV

*Your old life is dead. Your new life, which is your real life—even though invisible to spectators—is with Christ in God. He is your life.*

COLOSSIANS 3:3 MSG

## MORE POWERFUL IDEAS ABOUT THE PAST

Our yesterdays present irreparable things to us; it is true that we have lost opportunities which will never return, but God can transform this destructive anxiety into a constructive thoughtfulness for the future. Let the past sleep, but let it sleep on the bosom of Christ. Leave the Irreparable Past in His hands, and step out into the Irresistible Future with Him.

OSWALD CHAMBERS

We set our eyes on the finish line, forgetting the past, and straining toward the mark of spiritual maturity and fruitfulness.

VONETTE BRIGHT

Shake the dust from your past, and move forward in His promises.

KAY ARTHUR

God forgets the past. Imitate him.

MAX LUCADO

A TIP FOR TODAY

If you're focused on the past, change your focus. If you're living in the past, it's time to stop living there.

## A PRAYER FOR TODAY

*Heavenly Father, free me from anger, resentment, and envy. When I am bitter, I cannot feel the peace that You intend for my life. Keep me mindful that forgiveness is Your commandment, and help me accept the past, treasure the present, and trust the future . . . to You. Amen*

## TODAY'S THOUGHTS

My thoughts about the futility of focusing on past misfortunes.

_____

_____

_____

_____

_____

_____

_____

DAY 9

# TRUST GOD'S TIMING

*I waited patiently for the LORD;*
*and He inclined to me, and heard my cry.*

—

PSALM 40:1 NKJV

God knows not only what we need but also
when we need it. His timing is always perfect.

—

ELISABETH ELLIOT

The Bible teaches us to trust God's timing in all matters, but we are sorely tempted to do otherwise, especially when times are tough. When we are beset with problems, we are understandably anxious for a quick conclusion to our hardships. We know that our problems will end some day, and we want it to end NOW. God, however, works on His own timetable, and His schedule does not always coincide with ours.

God's plans are perfect; ours most certainly are not. So we must learn to trust the Father in good times and hard times. No exceptions.

Elisabeth Elliot advised, "We must learn to move according to the timetable of the Timeless One, and to be at peace." And Billy Graham observed, "As we wait on God, He helps us use the winds of adversity to soar above our problems."

So today, as you meet the challenges of everyday life, do your best to turn everything over to God. Whatever "it" is, He can handle it. And you can be sure that He will handle it when the time is right.

## PRAY FOR PATIENCE

Would you like to become a more patient person? Pray about it. Is there a person you dislike? Pray for a forgiving heart. Do you lose your temper more than you should? Ask God for help. Are you mired in the quicksand of regret? Ask God to liberate you.

As you pray more, you'll discover that God is always near and that He's always ready to hear from you. So don't worry about things; pray about them. God is waiting . . . and listening!

We must leave it to God to answer our prayers in
His own wisest way. Sometimes, we are so impatient
and think that God does not answer.
God always answers! He never fails!
Be still. Abide in Him.

MRS. CHARLES E. COWMAN

## MORE FROM GOD'S WORD ABOUT
## HIS TIMING

*Humble yourselves, therefore, under God's mighty hand, that he may lift you up in due time.*

1 PETER 5:6 NIV

*He told them, "You don't get to know the time. Timing is the Father's business."*

ACTS 1:7 MSG

*From one man he made every nation of men, that they should inhabit the whole earth; and he determined the times set for them and the exact places where they should live.*

ACTS 17:26 NIV

*There is a time for everything, and a season for every activity under heaven.*

ECCLESIASTES 3:1 NIV

*Yet the LORD longs to be gracious to you; he rises to show you compassion. For the LORD is a God of justice. Blessed are all who wait for him!*

ISAIAH 30:18 NIV

## MORE POWERFUL IDEAS ABOUT GOD'S TIMING

By his wisdom, he orders his delays so that they prove to be far better than our hurries.

C. H. SPURGEON

God is in no hurry. Compared to the works of mankind, He is extremely deliberate. God is not a slave to the human clock.

CHARLES SWINDOLL

Waiting on God brings us to the journey's end quicker than our feet.

MRS. CHARLES E. COWMAN

When we read of the great Biblical leaders, we see that it was not uncommon for God to ask them to wait, not just a day or two, but for years, until God was ready for them to act.

GLORIA GAITHER

### A TIP FOR TODAY

God is in control of His world and your world. Rely upon Him.

## A PRAYER FOR TODAY

*Dear Lord, Your timing is seldom my timing, but Your timing is always right for me. You are my Father, and You have a plan for my life that is grander than I can imagine. When I am impatient, remind me that You are never early or late. You are always on time, Lord, so let me trust in You . . . always. Amen*

## TODAY'S THOUGHTS

My thoughts about the need to trust God in all matters, including the time in which He chooses to reveal His plans and purposes.

DAY 10

# GOD DOES NOT CHANGE

*Be still, and know that I am God.*

—

PSALM 46:10 NKJV

> When all else is gone, God is still left.
> Nothing changes Him.
>
> —
>
> HANNAH WHITALL SMITH

These are times of great uncertainty. As we become accustomed to, and at times almost numbed by, a steady stream of unsettling news, we are reminded that our world is in a state of constant change. But God is not. So when the world seems to be trembling beneath our feet, we can be comforted in the knowledge that our Heavenly Father is the rock that cannot be shaken. His Word promises, "I am the Lord, I do not change" (Malachi 3:6 NKJV).

Every day that we live, we mortals encounter a multitude of changes—some good, some not so good. And on occasion, all of us must endure life-changing personal losses that leave us heartbroken. When we do, our Heavenly Father stands ready to comfort us, to guide us, and—in time—to heal us.

Is the world spinning a little too fast for your liking? Are you facing troubling uncertainties, difficult circumstances, or unwelcome changes? If so, please remember that God is far bigger than any problem you may face. So, instead of worrying about life's inevitable challenges, put your faith in the Father and His only begotten Son. After

all, "Jesus Christ is the same yesterday, today, and forever" (Hebrews 13:8 NKJV). And it is precisely because your Savior does not change that you can face your challenges with courage for today and hope for tomorrow.

Are you anxious about situations that you cannot control? Take your anxieties to God. Are you troubled? Take your troubles to Him. Does your little corner of the universe seem to be a frightening place? Seek protection from the One who cannot be moved. The same God who created the universe will protect you if you ask Him . . . so ask Him . . . and then serve Him with willing hands and a trusting heart.

He is within and without. His Spirit dwells within me.
His armor protects me.
He goes before me and is behind me.

—

MARY MORRISON SUGGS

## MORE FROM GOD'S WORD ABOUT HIS LOVE

*We know how much God loves us, and we have put our trust in him. God is love, and all who live in love live in God, and God lives in them.*

1 JOHN 4:16 NLT

*As the Father loved Me, I also have loved you; abide in My love.*

JOHN 15:9 NKJV

*The unfailing love of the LORD never ends! By his mercies we have been kept from complete destruction.*

LAMENTATIONS 3:22 NLT

*Whoever is wise will observe these things, and they will understand the lovingkindness of the Lord.*

PSALM 107:43 NKJV

*For God loved the world in this way: He gave His only Son, so that everyone who believes in Him will not perish but have eternal life.*

JOHN 3:16 HCSB

## MORE POWERFUL IDEAS ABOUT GOD'S PROTECTION

Under heaven's lock and key, we are protected by the most efficient security system available: the power of God.

CHARLES SWINDOLL

There is not only fear, but terrible danger, for the life unguarded by God.

OSWALD CHAMBERS

Once we recognize our need for Jesus, then the building of our faith begins. It is a daily, moment-by-moment life of absolute dependence upon Him for everything.

CATHERINE MARSHALL

The last and greatest lesson that the soul has to learn is the fact that God, and God alone, is enough for all its needs. This is the lesson that all His dealings with us are meant to teach; and this is the crowning discovery of our whole Christian life. God is enough!

HANNAH WHITALL SMITH

### A TIP FOR TODAY

God is here, and He wants to establish an intimate relationship with you. When you sincerely reach out to Him, you will sense His presence.

## A PRAYER FOR TODAY

*Dear Lord, Your love is eternal and Your laws are everlasting. When I obey Your commandments, I am blessed. Today, I invite You to reign over every corner of my heart. I will have faith in You, Father. I will sense Your presence; I will accept Your love; I will trust Your will; and I will praise You for the Savior of my life: Your Son, Jesus. Amen*

## TODAY'S THOUGHTS

My thoughts about God's power and His love.

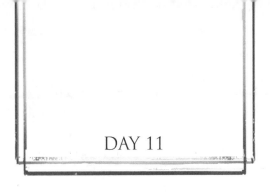

DAY 11

# ACCEPTING
# THE THINGS YOU
# CANNOT CHANGE

*For everything created by God is good,*
*and nothing should be rejected*
*if it is received with thanksgiving.*

—

1 TIMOTHY 4:4 HCSB

Acceptance says: True, this is my situation at
the moment. I'll look unblinkingly at the reality of it.
But, I'll also open my hands to accept willingly
whatever a loving Father sends me.

CATHERINE MARSHALL

Are you a woman who is embittered by an unexpected change or an unwelcome challenge that you did not deserve and cannot understand? If so, it's time to accept the unchangeable past and to have faith in the promise of tomorrow. It's time to trust God completely—and it's time to reclaim the peace—His peace—that can and should be yours.

On occasion, you will be confronted with situations that you simply don't understand. But God does. And He has a reason for everything that He does.

God doesn't explain Himself in ways that we, as mortals with limited insight and clouded vision, can comprehend. So, instead of understanding every aspect of God's unfolding plan for our lives and our universe, we must be satisfied to trust Him completely. We cannot know God's motivations, nor can we understand His actions. We can, however, trust Him, and we must.

## WHEN DREAMS DON'T COME TRUE

Some of our most important dreams are the ones we abandon. Some of our most important goals are the ones we don't attain. Sometimes, our most important journeys are the ones that we take to the winding conclusion of what seem to be dead-end streets. Thankfully, with God there are no dead-ends; there are only opportunities to learn, to yield, to trust, to serve, and to grow.

The next time you experience one of life's inevitable disappointments, don't despair and don't be afraid to try "Plan B." Consider every setback an opportunity to choose a different, more appropriate path. Have faith that God may indeed be leading you in an entirely different direction, a direction of His choosing. And as you take your next step, remember that what looks like a dead-end to you may, in fact, be the fast lane according to God.

Ultimately things work out best for those who make
the best of the way things work out.

—

BARBARA JOHNSON

## MORE FROM GOD'S WORD ABOUT
## ACCEPTANCE

*A man's heart plans his way, but the Lord determines his steps.*

PROVERBS 16:9 HCSB

*Do not remember the past events, pay no attention to things of old. Look, I am about to do something new; even now it is coming. Do you not see it? Indeed, I will make a way in the wilderness, rivers in the desert.*

ISAIAH 43:18-19 HCSB

*Should we accept only good from God and not adversity?*

JOB 2:10 HCSB

*Come to terms with God and be at peace; in this way good will come to you.*

JOB 22:21 HCSB

*Sheathe your sword! Should I not drink the cup that the Father has given Me?*

JOHN 18:11 HCSB

## MORE POWERFUL IDEAS ABOUT ACCEPTANCE

Surrender to the Lord is not a tremendous sacrifice, not an agonizing performance. It is the most sensible thing you can do.

CORRIE TEN BOOM

Acceptance is taking from God's hand absolutely anything He gives, looking into His face in trust and thanksgiving, knowing that the confinement of the situation we're in is good and for His glory.

CHARLES SWINDOLL

How changed our lives would be if we could only fly through the days on wings of surrender and trust!

HANNAH WHITALL SMITH

Tomorrow's job is fathered by today's acceptance. Acceptance of what, at least for the moment, you cannot alter.

MAX LUCADO

### A TIP FOR TODAY

Sometimes, the blessings God gives us are not the ones we've asked for. But even when we cannot understand God's plan for our lives, we should be thankful for His eternal perspective and His eternal love.

## A PRAYER FOR TODAY

*Father, the events of this world unfold according to a plan that I cannot fully understand. But You understand. Help me to trust You, Lord, even when I am grieving. Help me to trust You even when I am confused. Today, in whatever circumstances I find myself, let me trust Your will and accept Your love . . . completely. Amen*

## TODAY'S THOUGHTS

My thoughts about the things I cannot change.

_____

_____

_____

_____

_____

_____

_____

_____

DAY 12

# GOD HAS A PLAN FOR YOU

*Who are those who fear the Lord?*
*He will show them the path they should choose.*
*They will live in prosperity, and their children*
*will inherit the Promised Land.*

—

PSALM 25:12-13 NLT

With God, it's never "Plan B" or "second best."
It's always "Plan A." And, if we let Him,
He'll make something beautiful of our lives.

—

GLORIA GAITHER

It's an age-old riddle: Why does God allow us to endure tough times? After all, since we trust that God is all-powerful, and since we trust that His hand shapes our lives, why doesn't He simply rescue us—and our loved ones—from all hardship and pain?

God's Word teaches us again and again that He loves us and wants the best for us. And the Bible also teaches us that God is ever-present and always watchful. So why, we wonder, if God is really so concerned with every detail of our lives, does He permit us to endure emotions like grief, sadness, shame, or fear? And why does He allow tragic circumstances to invade the lives of good people? These questions perplex us, especially when times are tough.

On occasion, all of us face adversity, and throughout life, we all must endure life-changing personal losses that leave us breathless. When we pass through the dark valleys of life, we often ask, "Why me?" Sometimes, of course, the answer is obvious—sometimes we make mistakes, and we must pay for them. But on other occasions, when we

have done nothing wrong, we wonder why God allows us to suffer.

Even when we cannot understand God's plans, we must trust them. And even when we are impatient for our situations to improve, we must trust God's timing. If we seek to live in accordance with His plan for our lives, we must continue to study His Word (in good times and bad), and we must be watchful for His signs, knowing that in time, He will lead us through the valleys, onward to the mountaintop.

So, if you're a woman who is enduring tough times, don't give up and don't give in. God still has glorious plans for you. So keep your eyes and ears open . . . as well as your heart.

## FINDING NEW MEANING

Perhaps tough times have turned your world upside down. Maybe it seems to you as if everything in your life has been rearranged. Or perhaps your relationships and your responsibilities have been permanently altered. If so, you may come face to face with the daunting task of finding new purpose for your life. And God is willing to help.

God has an important plan for your life, and part of His plan may well be related to the tough times you're

experiencing. After all, you've learned important, albeit hard-earned, lessons. And you're certainly wiser today than you were yesterday. So your suffering carries with it great potential: the potential for intense personal growth and the potential to help others.

As you begin to reorganize your life, look for ways to use your experiences for the betterment of others. When you do, you can rest assured that the course of your recovery will depend upon how quickly you discover new people to help and new reasons to live. And as you move through and beyond your own particular tough times, be mindful of this fact: as a survivor, you will have countless opportunities to serve others. By serving others, you will bring glory to God and meaning to the hardships you've endured.

*It is God who works in you to will and to act according to his good purpose.*

—

PHILIPPIANS 2:13 NIV

## MORE FROM GOD'S WORD ABOUT
## HIS PLAN

*"For I know the plans I have for you," declares the Lord, "plans to prosper you and not to harm you, plans to give you hope and a future. Then you will call upon me and come and pray to me, and I will listen to you."*

JEREMIAH 29:11-12 NIV

*And we know that in all things God works for the good of those who love him, who have been called according to his purpose.*

ROMANS 8:28 NIV

*He replied, "Every plant that My heavenly Father didn't plant will be uprooted."*

MATTHEW 15:13 HCSB

*The steps of the Godly are directed by the Lord. He delights in every detail of their lives. Though they stumble, they will not fall, for the Lord holds them by the hand.*

PSALM 37:23-24 NLT

## MORE POWERFUL IDEAS ABOUT GOD'S PLAN

Every misfortune, every failure, every loss may be transformed. God has the power to transform all misfortunes into "God-sends."

MRS. CHARLES E. COWMAN

Our loving God uses difficulty in our lives to burn away the sin of self and build faith and spiritual power.

BILL BRIGHT

On the darkest day of your life, God is still in charge. Take comfort in that.

MARIE T. FREEMAN

### A TIP FOR TODAY

Waiting faithfully for God's plan to unfold is more important than understanding God's plan. So, you must trust Him and never lose faith!

Don't let circumstances distress you. Rather, look for the will of God for your life to be revealed in and through those circumstances.

BILLY GRAHAM

## A PRAYER FOR TODAY

*Dear Lord, even when I am discouraged, even when my heart is heavy, I will earnestly seek Your will for my life. You have a plan for me that I can never fully understand. But You understand. And I will trust You today, tomorrow, and forever. Amen*

## TODAY'S THOUGHTS

My thoughts about the importance of understanding life lessons and using them to follow God's plan for my life.

DAY 13

# THE POWER OF PRAYER

*Is anyone among you suffering? He should pray.
Is anyone cheerful? He should sing praises.*

—

JAMES 5:13 HCSB

I have found the perfect antidote for fear.
Whenever it sticks up its ugly face,
I clobber it with prayer.

—

DALE EVANS ROGERS

God is trying to get His message through . . . to you! Are you listening?

Perhaps, if you're experiencing tough times, you may find yourself overwhelmed by the pressure of everyday life. Perhaps you forget to slow yourself down long enough to talk with God. Instead of turning your thoughts and prayers to Him, you may rely upon our own resources. Instead of asking God for guidance, you may depend only upon your own limited wisdom. A far better course of action is this: simply stop what you're doing long enough to open your heart to God; then listen carefully for His directions.

Do you spend time each day with God? You should. Are you in need? Ask God to sustain you. Are you troubled? Take your worries to Him in prayer. Are you weary? Seek God's strength. In all things great and small, seek God's wisdom and His grace. He hears your prayers, and He will answer. All you must do is ask.

## GOT QUESTIONS?

You've got questions? God's got answers. And if you'd like to hear from Him, here's precisely what you must do: petition Him with a sincere heart; be still; be patient; and listen. Then, in His own time and in His own fashion, God will answer your questions and give you guidance for the journey ahead.

Today, turn over everything to your Creator. Pray constantly about matters great and small. Seek God's instruction and His direction. And remember: God hears your prayers and answers them. But He won't answer the prayers that you don't get around to praying. So pray early and often. And then wait patiently for answers that are sure to come.

## MORE FROM GOD'S WORD ABOUT PRAYER

*"Relax, Daniel," he continued, "don't be afraid. From the moment you decided to humble yourself to receive understanding, your prayer was heard, and I set out to come to you."*

DANIEL 10:12 MSG

*If you don't know what you're doing, pray to the Father. He loves to help. You'll get his help, and won't be condescended to when you ask for it. Ask boldly, believingly, without a second thought. People who "worry their prayers" are like windwhipped waves. Don't think you're going to get anything from the Master that way, adrift at sea, keeping all your options open.*

JAMES 1:5-8 MSG

*Rejoice always, pray without ceasing, in everything give thanks; for this is the will of God in Christ Jesus for you.*

1 THESSALONIANS 5:16-18 NKJV

*I want men everywhere to lift up holy hands in prayer, without anger or disputing.*

1 TIMOTHY 2:8 NIV

## MORE POWERFUL IDEAS ABOUT PRAYER

The center of power is not to be found in summit meetings or in peace conferences. It is not in Peking or Washington or the United Nations, but rather where a child of God prays in the power of the Spirit for God's will to be done in her life, in her home, and in the world around her.

RUTH BELL GRAHAM

I have witnessed many attitudes make a positive turn-around through prayer.

JOHN MAXWELL

Real power in prayer flows only when a man's spirit touches God's spirit.

CATHERINE MARSHALL

### A TIP FOR TODAY

God does not answer all of our prayers in the affirmative, nor should He. His job is not to grant all our earthly requests; His job is to offer us eternal salvation.

Any concern that is too small to be turned into a prayer is too small to be made into a burden.

CORRIE TEN BOOM

## A PRAYER FOR TODAY

*Dear Lord, make me a woman of constant prayer. Your Holy Word commands me to pray without ceasing. In all things great and small, at all times, whether happy or sad, let me seek Your wisdom and Your strength . . . in prayer. Amen*

## TODAY'S THOUGHTS

My thoughts about the role that prayer does play—and should play—in the way that I meet life's challenges.

_____

_____

_____

_____

_____

_____

_____

_____

_____

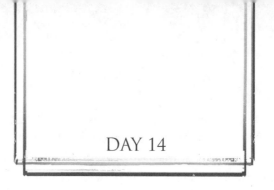

DAY 14

# FINDING SAFETY IN GOD'S WORD

*All Scripture is inspired by God and is profitable for*
*teaching, for rebuking, for correcting, for training*
*in righteousness, so that the man of God may be*
*complete, equipped for every good work.*

—

2 TIMOTHY 3:16-17 HCSB

God can see clearly no matter
how dark or foggy the night is.
Trust His Word to guide you safely home.

—

LISA WHELCHEL

God's promises are found in a book like no other: the Holy Bible. The Bible is a road map for life here on earth and for life eternal. As Christians, we are called upon to trust its promises, to follow its commandments, and to share its Good News.

As believers, we must study the Bible each day and meditate upon its meaning for our lives. Otherwise, we deprive ourselves of a priceless gift from our Creator. God's Holy Word is, indeed, a transforming, life-changing, one-of-a-kind treasure. And, a passing acquaintance with the Good Book is insufficient for Christians who seek to obey God's Word and to understand His will.

God has made promises to mankind and to you. God's promises never fail and they never grow old. You must trust those promises and share them with your family, with your friends, and with the world.

Are you standing on the promises of God? Are you expecting God to protect you today and every day, or are you living beneath a cloud of apprehension and doubt? The familiar words of Psalm 118:24 remind us of a profound

yet simple truth: "This is the day which the LORD hath made; we will rejoice and be glad in it" (KJV). Do you trust that promise, and do you live accordingly? If so, you are living the passionate life that God intends.

For passionate believers, every day begins and ends with God's Son and God's promises. When we accept Christ into our hearts, God promises us the opportunity for earthly peace and spiritual abundance. But more importantly, God promises us the priceless gift of eternal life.

As we face the inevitable challenges of life-here-on-earth, we must arm ourselves with the promises of God's Holy Word. When we do, we can expect the best, not only for the day ahead, but also for all eternity.

## GOD'S WORD REDUCES STRESS

If you're experiencing stress, God's Word can help relieve it. And if you'd like to experience God's peace, Bible study can help provide it.

Warren Wiersbe observed, "When the child of God looks into the Word of God, he sees the Son of God. And, he is transformed by the Spirit of God to share in the glory of God." God's Holy Word is, indeed, a life-changing, stress-reducing, one-of-a-kind treasure. And it's up to you—and only you—to use it that way.

## MORE FROM GOD'S WORD ABOUT THE BIBLE

*This is my comfort in my affliction, for Your word has given me life.*

PSALM 119:50 NKJV

*But the word of the Lord endures forever. And this is the word that was preached as the gospel to you.*

1 PETER 1:25 HCSB

*Let the Word of Christ—the Message—have the run of the house. Give it plenty of room in your lives. Instruct and direct one another using good common sense. And sing, sing your hearts out to God! Let every detail in your lives—words, actions, whatever—be done in the name of the Master, Jesus, thanking God the Father every step of the way.*

COLOSSIANS 3:16-17 MSG

*For the word of God is living and active. Sharper than any double-edged sword, it penetrates even to dividing soul and spirit, joints and marrow; it judges the thoughts and attitudes of the heart.*

HEBREWS 4:12 NIV

## MORE POWERFUL IDEAS ABOUT GOD'S WORD

Weave the unveiling fabric of God's word through your heart and mind. It will hold strong, even if the rest of life unravels.

GIGI GRAHAM TCHIVIDJIAN

The strength that we claim from God's Word does not depend on circumstances. Circumstances will be difficult, but our strength will be sufficient.

CORRIE TEN BOOM

Nobody ever outgrows Scripture; the book widens and deepens with our years.

C. H. SPURGEON

### A TIP FOR TODAY

Take a Bible with you wherever you go. You never know when you may need a midday spiritual pick-me-up.

The Bible is God's Word, given to us by God Himself so we can know Him and His will for our lives.

BILLY GRAHAM

## A PRAYER FOR TODAY

*Heavenly Father, Your Word is a light unto the world; I will study it and trust it and share it. In all that I do, help me be a worthy witness for You as I share the Good News of Your perfect Son and Your perfect Word. Amen*

## TODAY'S THOUGHTS

My thoughts about the rewards of regular Bible study.

_____

_____

_____

_____

_____

_____

_____

_____

_____

_____

DAY 15

# OVERCOMING TEMPTATION

*No temptation has overtaken you except what is common to humanity. God is faithful and He will not allow you to be tempted beyond what you are able, but with the temptation He will also provide a way of escape, so that you are able to bear it.*

—

1 CORINTHIANS 10:13 HCSB

God builds us up so we can withstand attacks from
temptation in the world, from Satan,
and from our own fleshly desires.

—

VONETTE BRIGHT

I t's inevitable: today you will be tempted by somebody
or something—in fact, you will probably be tempted
on countless occasions. Why? Because you live in a
world that's filled to the brim with temptations and addictions that are intended to lead you far, far away from God.

Here in the 21st century, temptations are now completely and thoroughly woven into the fabric of everyday
life. Seductive images are everywhere; subtle messages tell
you that it's okay to sin "just a little"; and to make matters
even worse, society doesn't just seem to endorse godless-
ness, it actually seems to reward it. Society spews forth a
wide range of messages, all of which imply that it's okay
to rebel against God. These messages, of course, are extremely dangerous and completely untrue.

How can you stand up against society's tidal wave of
temptations? By learning to direct your thoughts and your
eyes in ways that are pleasing to God . . . and by rely-
ing upon Him to deliver you from the evils that threaten
you. And here's the good news: the Creator has promised (not implied, not suggested, not insinuated—He has

promised!) that with His help, you can resist every single temptation that confronts you.

When it comes to fighting Satan, you are never alone. God is always with you, and if you do your part He will do His part. But what, precisely, is your part? A good starting point is simply learning how to recognize the subtle temptations that surround you. The images of immorality are ubiquitous, and they're intended to hijack your mind, your heart, your pocketbook, your life, and your soul. Don't let them do it.

Satan is both industrious and creative; he's working 24/7, and he's causing pain, heartache, trauma, and tragedy in more ways than ever before. You, as woman of God, must remain watchful and strong—starting today and ending never.

> Because Christ has faced our every temptation
> without sin, we never face a temptation
> that has no door of escape.
>
> —
>
> BETH MOORE

# MORE FROM GOD'S WORD ABOUT
# TEMPTATION

*Be sober! Be on the alert! Your adversary the Devil is prowling around like a roaring lion, looking for anyone he can devour.*

1 PETER 5:8 HCSB

*Put on the full armor of God so that you can stand against the tactics of the Devil.*

EPHESIANS 6:11 HCSB

*Stay awake and pray, so that you won't enter into temptation. The spirit is willing, but the flesh is weak.*

MATTHEW 26:41 HCSB

*The Spirit's law of life in Christ Jesus has set you free from the law of sin and of death.*

ROMANS 8:2 HCSB

*Do not be deceived: "Bad company corrupts good morals."*

1 CORINTHIANS 15:33 HCSB

## MORE POWERFUL IDEAS ABOUT TEMPTATION

Do not fight the temptation in detail. Turn from it. Look ONLY at your Lord. Sing. Read. Work.

AMY CARMICHAEL

Temptation is not a sin. Even Jesus was tempted. The Lord Jesus gives you the strength needed to resist temptation.

CORRIE TEN BOOM

In the Garden of Gethsemane, Jesus went through agony of soul in His efforts to resist the temptation to do what He felt like doing rather than what He knew was God's will for Him.

JOYCE MEYER

### A TIP FOR TODAY

Because you live in a temptation-filled world, you must guard your eyes, your thoughts, and your heart—all day, every day.

The devil's most devilish when respectable.

ELIZABETH BARRETT
BROWNING

## A PRAYER FOR TODAY

*Dear Lord, this world is filled with temptations, distractions, and frustrations. When I turn my thoughts away from You and Your Word, Lord, I suffer bitter consequences. But, when I trust in Your commandments, I am safe. Direct my path far from the temptations and distractions of the world. Let me discover Your will and follow it, Dear Lord, this day and always. Amen*

## TODAY'S THOUGHTS

My thoughts about the dangers of the world's distractions and temptations.

_____

_____

_____

_____

_____

_____

_____

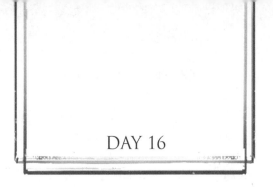

# WHY MUST WE ENDURE CHALLENGING TIMES?

*Should we accept only good from God
and not adversity?*

—

JOB 2:10 HCSB

Every experience God gives us, every person
He brings into our lives, is the perfect preparation
for the future that only He can see.

—

CORRIE TEN BOOM

God's Word teaches us over and over again that He loves us and wants the best for us. It also teaches us that God is ever-present and always watchful. So why, we wonder, if God is really so concerned with every detail of our lives, does He permit us to endure challenges that make us feel emotions like grief, sadness, shame, or fear? Why does He allow tragic circumstances to invade the lives of good people? Why, we wonder, does God insist upon throwing us curveballs when we would prefer that He slowly lob softballs right over the center of the plate?

The answers to these questions reveals certain truths about our Creator and about ourselves. We human beings are creatures of free will. We make countless choices every day: some wise, some not-so-wise, and some downright foolish. When we make bad choices, we are not always punished immediately, but if we make enough bad choices—and if we keep making them over and over again—we're bound to reap the bitter harvest that we've sown. It's a matter of cause and effect.

Simply put, God has created a world in which good behavior is rewarded and bad behavior is not. So when we disobey God's tenets, or when we ignore the quiet voice of conscience that He has placed within our hearts, we must eventually suffer the consequences of our shortsightedness. In such circumstances, we have no right—or reason—to blame God.

But what are we to think when nobody is to blame? What are we to surmise when we've tried hard to do the right thing but have received only heartbreak in return? Or what about those instances when dreadful things happen to totally innocent victims? What are we to do when life seems totally unfair and God seems totally uninvolved? These situations present thornier problems because we see no apparent cause that might account for the unwelcome turn of events. During these darker moments, we learn something important about God: He is not required, nor does He intend, to explain Himself in ways that we, as mere mortals, might prefer. God is not in the business of answering all our questions now, but He has promised to answer them some day in heaven. And until that wonderful day arrives, we must learn to trust the Creator even though we cannot understand Him.

In the book of Job, we are told of a man who was thoroughly tested by God. Job was a wealthy farmer, a godly father with a large family, an upstanding man who had done nothing to earn God's wrath. But Satan came before

God to claim that Job's godliness was a result of prosperity, not genuine righteousness. So God allowed Satan to strip Job of his wealth, his children, and his health.

After these tragedies had befallen Job, he was visited by three friends who mistakenly assumed that Job's suffering was the result of sin. The friends believed that Job must have disobeyed God; otherwise, they surmised, God would never punish Job so severely. The friends, of course, were wrong; in truth, they were simply incapable of knowing God's intentions, as are we.

Despite his sufferings, Job refused to "curse God and die" (Job 2:9). Instead, he remained steadfast in his faith. Finally, "the Lord blessed the latter part of Job's life more than the first" (Job 42:12 NIV). God restored Job's wealth and health—and He gave Job ten more children. But God never fully explained Himself to Job. To the contrary, God warned Job that His divine motivations were then—as they are now—beyond human understanding.

If God has thrown you (or your loved one) a tough pitch to hit, or if He has allowed someone else's transgressions to bring pain into your life, then you, like Job, may ask, "Why?" Sometimes God will answer that question, and sometimes He will not. In either event, you must respect the Creator's infinite power, and you must learn to trust Him completely. After all, He has promised to lift you up, to protect you, to give you strength, and to renew your spirits . . . if you let Him.

At times, you'll undoubtedly be assaulted by feelings of bitterness and regret. But God intends that you rise above those feelings, and that's precisely what you should strive to do. The sooner you let go of the past, the sooner you can embrace your future.

So remember: God reigns over the entire universe and He reigns over your little corner of that universe. He is sovereign. Your challenge is to recognize God's sovereignty and to live in accordance with His commandments, no matter your circumstances.

Your Heavenly Father may not always reveal Himself as quickly or as clearly as you would like. But rest assured: God is in control, God is here, and God intends to use you in wonderful, unexpected ways. He desires to lead you along a path of His choosing. Your challenge is to watch, to listen, to learn . . . and to follow.

## MORE FROM GOD'S WORD ABOUT
## HIS SOVEREIGNTY

*For now we see indistinctly, as in a mirror, but then face to face. Now I know in part, but then I will know fully, as I am fully known.*

1 CORINTHIANS 13:12 HCSB

*However, each one must live his life in the situation the Lord assigned when God called him.*

1 CORINTHIANS 7:17 HCSB

*O Lord, you have examined my heart and know everything about me. You know when I sit down or stand up. You know my every thought when far away. You chart the path ahead of me and tell me where to stop and rest.*

PSALM 139:1-3 NLT

*Ah, Lord God! Behold, You have made the heavens and the earth by Your great power and outstretched arm. There is nothing too hard for You.*

JEREMIAH 32:17 NKJV

## MORE POWERFUL IDEAS ABOUT OVERCOMING CHALLENGES

Nothing happens by happenstance. I am not in the hands of fate, nor am I the victim of man's whims or the devil's ploys. There is One who sits above man, above Satan, and above all heavenly hosts as the ultimate authority of all the universe. That One is my God and my Father!

KAY ARTHUR

As you place yourself under the sovereign lordship of Jesus Christ, each mistake or failure can lead you right back to the throne.

BARBARA JOHNSON

### A TIP FOR TODAY

God is in control of His world and your world. Rely upon Him.

We do not understand the intricate pattern of the stars in their course, but we know that He Who created them does, and that just as surely as He guides them, He is charting a safe course for us.

BILLY GRAHAM

## A PRAYER FOR TODAY

*Dear Lord, when I am fearful, keep me mindful that You are my protector and my salvation. Thank You, Father, for a perfect love that casts out fear. Because of You, I can live courageously and faithfully this day and every day. Amen*

## TODAY'S THOUGHTS

My thoughts about the need to trust God in every situation.

_____

_____

_____

_____

_____

_____

_____

_____

_____

_____

DAY 17

# BEYOND ANXIETY

*Don't worry about anything, but in everything,
through prayer and petition with thanksgiving,
let your requests be made known to God.*

—

PHILIPPIANS 4:6 HCSB

We must lay our questions, frustrations, anxieties, and impotence at the feet of God and wait for His answer. And then receiving it, we must live by faith.

—

KAY ARTHUR

We live in a world that sometimes seems to shift beneath our feet. We live in a dangerous world, a world where tragedies can befall even the most godly among us. And we are members of an anxious society, a society in which the changes we face threaten to outpace our abilities to make adjustments. No wonder we sometimes find ourselves beset by feelings of anxiety and panic.

At times, our anxieties may stem from physical causes—chemical imbalances in the brain that result in severe emotional distress or relentless panic attacks. In such cases, modern medicine offers hope to those who suffer. But oftentimes, our anxieties result from spiritual deficits, not physical ones. And when we're spiritually depleted, the best prescription is found not in the medicine cabinet but deep inside the human heart. What we need is a higher daily dose of God's love, God's peace, God's assurance, and God's presence. And how do we acquire these blessings from our Creator? Through prayer, through meditation, through worship, and through trust.

Prayer is a powerful antidote to anxiety; so, too, is a regular time of devotional reading and meditation. When we spend quiet moments in the divine presence of our Heavenly Father, we are reminded once again that our troubles are temporary but His love is not.

Worship, like prayer, is another tool that can help us overcome the worries and doubts of our anxious age. When we worship God sincerely with our words, with our thoughts, with our prayers, and with our deeds, we are blessed. But the reverse is also true: when we fail to worship God, for whatever reason, we forfeit the spiritual gifts that He intends to be ours.

Learning to trust God completely and without reservation is yet another antidote to anxiety. In fact, a fundamental relationship exists between anxiety and trust: the more we trust God, the less anxious we are likely to feel. But once again, the reverse is also true: the less we trust God, the more anxious we are likely to become. When we turn away from God and rely, instead, upon the world for our deliverance, we will be troubled—and rightfully so. The world will disappoint us; God will not.

From time to time, all of us face life-changing personal losses that leave us breathless. When we do, God stands ready to protect us. Psalm 147 promises, "He heals the brokenhearted and bandages their wounds" (v. 3, NCV). When we are troubled, we must call upon God, and, in His own time and according to His own plan, He will heal us.

Are you anxious? Take those anxieties to God. Are you troubled? Take your troubles to Him. Does your world seem to be trembling beneath your feet? Seek protection from the One who cannot be moved. The same God who created the universe will protect you if you ask Him . . . so ask and trust.

Worry and anxiety are sand in the machinery of life;
faith is the oil.

—

E. STANLEY JONES

## MORE FROM GOD'S WORD ABOUT
## TRUSTING HIM MORE AND WORRYING LESS

*Therefore don't worry about tomorrow, because tomorrow will worry about itself. Each day has enough trouble of its own.*

MATTHEW 6:34 HCSB

*Anxiety in a man's heart weighs it down, but a good word cheers it up.*

PROVERBS 12:25 HCSB

*Why am I so depressed? Why this turmoil within me? Put your hope in God, for I will still praise Him, my Savior and my God.*

PSALM 42:11 HCSB

*In the multitude of my anxieties within me, Your comforts delight my soul.*

PSALM 94:19 NKJV

*So I say to you, keep asking, and it will be given to you. Keep searching, and you will find. Keep knocking, and the door will be opened to you.*

LUKE 11:9 HCSB

## MORE POWERFUL IDEAS ABOUT OVERCOMING ANXIETY

So often we pray and then fret anxiously, waiting for God to hurry up and do something. All the while God is waiting for us to calm down, so He can do something through us.

CORRIE TEN BOOM

Never yield to gloomy anticipation. Place your hope and confidence in God. He has no record of failure.

MRS. CHARLES E. COWMAN

Worry is the senseless process of cluttering up tomorrow's opportunities with leftover problems from today.

BARBARA JOHNSON

Are you serious about wanting God's guidance to become the person he wants you to be? The first step is to tell God that you know you can't manage your own life; that you need his help.

CATHERINE MARSHALL

### A TIP FOR TODAY

Focus on your work, not your worries. Worry is never a valid substitute for work, so get busy, do your best, and turn your worries over to God.

## A PRAYER FOR TODAY

*Lord, sometimes this world is a difficult place, and, as a frail human being, I am fearful. When I am worried, restore my faith. When I am anxious, turn my thoughts to You. When I grieve, touch my heart with Your enduring love. Give me the wisdom to trust in You, Father, and give me the courage to live a life of faith, not a life of fear. Amen*

## TODAY'S THOUGHTS

My thoughts about the security of God's love and the certainty of His promises.

_____

_____

_____

_____

_____

_____

_____

_____

DAY 18

# SELF-ESTEEM
# ACCORDING TO GOD

*For you made us only a little lower than God,*
*and you crowned us with glory and honor.*

—

PSALM 8:5 NLT

Being loved by Him whose opinion matters most gives us the security to risk loving, too—even loving ourselves.

—

GLORIA GAITHER

When you encounter tough times, you may lose self-confidence. Or you may become so focused on what other people are thinking—or saying—that you fail to focus on God. To do so is a mistake of major proportions—don't make it. Instead, seek God's guidance as you focus your energies on becoming the best you that you can possibly be. And when it comes to matters of self-esteem and self-image, seek approval not from your peers, but from your Creator.

Millions of words have been written about various ways to improve self-image and increase self-esteem. Yet, maintaining a healthy self-image is, to a surprising extent, a matter of doing three things: 1. obeying God, 2. thinking healthy thoughts, 3. finding a purpose for your life that pleases your Creator and yourself. The following common-sense, Biblically-based tips can help you build the kind of self-image—and the kind of life—that both you and God can be proud of:

1. Do the right thing: If you're misbehaving, how can you possibly hope to feel good about yourself? (Romans 14:12)

2. Watch what you think: If your inner voice is, in reality, your inner critic, you need to tone down the criticism now. And while you're at it, train yourself to begin thinking thoughts that are more rational, more accepting, and less judgmental. (Philippians 4:8)

3. Spend time with boosters, not critics: Are your friends putting you down? If so, find new friends. (Hebrews 3:13)

4. Don't be a perfectionist: Strive for excellence, but never confuse it with perfection. (Ecclesiastes 11:4,6)

5. If you're addicted to something unhealthy, stop; if you can't stop, get help: Addictions, of whatever type, create havoc in your life. And disorder. And grief. And low self-esteem. (Exodus 20:3)

6. Find a purpose for your life that is larger than you are: When you're dedicated to something or someone besides yourself, you blossom. (Ephesians 6:7)

7. Don't worry too much about self-esteem: Instead, worry more about living a life that is pleasing to God Learn to think optimistically. Find a worthy purpose. Find people to love and people to serve. When you do, your self-esteem will, on most days, take care of itself.

## MORE FROM GOD'S WORD ABOUT
## YOUR SELF-WORTH

*You're blessed when you're content with just who you are—no more, no less. That's the moment you find yourselves proud owners of everything that can't be bought.*

MATTHEW 5:5 MSG

*A devout life does bring wealth, but it's the rich simplicity of being yourself before God.*

1 TIMOTHY 6:6 MSG

*You made all the delicate, inner parts of my body and knit me together in my mother's womb. Thank you for making me so wonderfully complex! Your workmanship is marvelous—and how well I know it.*

PSALM 139:13-14 NLT

*My dear children, let's not just talk about love; let's practice real love. This is the only way we'll know we're living truly, living in God's reality. It's also the way to shut down debilitating self-criticism, even when there is something to it. For God is greater than our worried hearts and knows more about us than we do ourselves. And friends, once that's taken care of and we're no longer accusing or condemning ourselves, we're bold and free before God!*

1 JOHN 3:18-21 MSG

## MORE POWERFUL IDEAS ABOUT SELF-WORTH

As you and I lay up for ourselves living, lasting treasures in Heaven, we come to the awesome conclusion that we ourselves are His treasure!

ANNE GRAHAM LOTZ

The Creator has made us each one of a kind. There is nobody else exactly like us, and there never will be. Each of us is his special creation and is alive for a distinctive purpose.

LUCI SWINDOLL

Comparison is the root of all feelings of inferiority.

JAMES DOBSON

When it comes to our position before God, we're perfect. When he sees each of us, he sees one who has been made perfect through the One who is perfect—Jesus Christ.

MAX LUCADO

### A TIP FOR TODAY

No matter the size of your challenges, you can be sure that you and God, working together, can tackle them.

## A PRAYER FOR TODAY

*Dear Lord, help me speak courteously to everyone, including myself. And when I make a mistake, help me to forgive myself quickly and thoroughly, just as I forgive others. Amen*

## TODAY'S THOUGHTS

My thoughts about the importance of maintaining a positive self-image and an optimistic outlook on life.

_____

_____

_____

_____

_____

_____

_____

_____

_____

_____

DAY 19

# DON'T GIVE UP!

*No matter how many times you trip them up,*
*God-loyal people don't stay down long;*
*Soon they're up on their feet,*
*while the wicked end up flat on their faces.*

—

PROVERBS 24:16 MSG

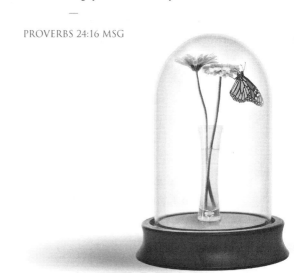

Failure is one of life's most powerful teachers.
How we handle our failures determines whether we're
going to simply "get by" in life or "press on."

—

BETH MOORE

The old saying is as true today as it was when it was first spoken: "Life is a marathon, not a sprint." That's why wise travelers (like you) select a traveling companion who never tires and never falters. That partner, of course, is your Heavenly Father.

The next time you find your courage tested by an unwelcome change, remember that God is as near as your next breath, and remember that He offers strength and comfort to His children. He is your shield and your strength; He is your protector and your deliverer. Call upon Him in your hour of need and then be comforted. Whatever your challenge, whatever your trouble, God can help you persevere. And that's precisely what He'll do if you ask Him.

Perhaps you are in a hurry for God to help you resolve your challenges. Perhaps you're anxious to earn the rewards that you feel you've already earned from life. Perhaps you're drumming your fingers, impatiently waiting for God to act. If so, be forewarned: God operates on His own timetable, not yours. Sometimes, God may answer your prayers with silence, and when He does, you must patient-

ly persevere. In times of trouble, you must remain steadfast and trust in the merciful goodness of your Heavenly Father. Whatever your problem, He can handle it. Your job is to keep persevering until He does.

## LOOK TO JESUS

In a world filled with roadblocks and stumbling blocks, we need strength, courage, and perseverance. And, as an example of perfect perseverance, we need look no further than our Savior, Jesus Christ.

Jesus finished what He began. Despite the torture He endured, despite the shame of the cross, Jesus was steadfast in His faithfulness to God. We, too, must remain faithful, especially during times of hardship.

As you navigate the inevitable changes of modern-day life, you will undoubtedly experience your fair share of disappointments, detours, false starts, and failures. When you do, don't become discouraged: God's not finished with you yet.

We are all on our way somewhere.
We'll get there if we just keep going.

—

BARBARA JOHNSON

## MORE FROM GOD'S WORD ABOUT
### PERSEVERANCE

*Let us not become weary in doing good, for at the proper time we will reap a harvest if we do not give up.*

GALATIANS 6:9 NIV

*For you have need of endurance, so that when you have done the will of God, you may receive what was promised.*

HEBREWS 10:36 NASB

*Thanks be to God! He gives us the victory through our Lord Jesus Christ. Therefore, my dear brothers, stand firm. Let nothing move you. Always give yourselves fully to the work of the Lord, because you know that your labor in the Lord is not in vain.*

1 CORINTHIANS 15:57-58 NIV

*Be diligent that ye may be found of him in peace, without spot, and blameless.*

2 PETER 3:14 KJV

*It is better to finish something than to start it. It is better to be patient than to be proud.*

ECCLESIASTES 7:8 NCV

## MORE POWERFUL IDEAS ABOUT PERSEVERANCE

We don't give up. We look up. We trust. We believe. And our optimism is not hollow. Christ has proven worthy. He has shown that he never fails. That's what makes God, God.

MAX LUCADO

Are you a Christian? If you are, how can you be hopeless? Are you so depressed by the greatness of your problems that you have given up all hope? Instead of giving up, would you patiently endure? Would you focus on Christ until you are so preoccupied with him alone that you fall prostrate before him?

ANNE GRAHAM LOTZ

Just remember, every flower that ever bloomed had to go through a whole lot of dirt to get there!

BARBARA JOHNSON

### A TIP FOR TODAY

If things don't work out at first, don't quit. If you don't keep trying, you'll never know how good you can be.

## A PRAYER FOR TODAY

*Lord, when life is difficult, I am tempted to abandon hope in the future. But You are my God, and I can draw strength from You. Let me trust You, Father, in good times and in bad times. Let me persevere—even if my soul is troubled—and let me follow Your Son, Jesus Christ, this day and forever. Amen*

## TODAY'S THOUGHTS

My thoughts about the power of perseverance.

_____

_____

_____

_____

_____

_____

_____

_____

DAY 20

# RENEWED DAY BY DAY

*Every morning he wakes me.*
*He teaches me to listen like a student.*
*The Lord God helps me learn . . .*

—

ISAIAH 50:4-5 NCV

Jesus challenges you and me
to keep our focus daily on the cross of His will
if we want to be His disciples.

—

ANNE GRAHAM LOTZ

Each new day is a gift from God, and if you are wise, you will spend a few quiet moments each morning thanking the Giver. When you do, you'll discover that time spent with God can lift your spirits and relieve your stress.

Warren Wiersbe writes, "Surrender your mind to the Lord at the beginning of each day." And that's sound advice. When you begin each day with your head bowed and your heart lifted, you are reminded of God's love, His protection, and His commandments. Then, you can align your priorities for the coming day with the teachings and commandments that God has placed upon your heart.

So, if you've acquired the unfortunate habit of trying to "squeeze" God into the corners of your life, it's time to reshuffle the items on your to-do list by placing God first. And if you haven't already done so, form the habit of spending quality time with your Father in heaven. He deserves it . . . and so do you.

## PRAY ABOUT IT

Andrew Murray observed, "Some people pray just to pray, and some people pray to know God." Your task, as a maturing believer, is to pray, not out of habit or obligation, but out of a sincere desire to know your Heavenly Father. Through constant prayers, you should petition God, you should praise Him, and you should seek to discover His unfolding plans for your life.

Today, reach out to the Giver of all blessings. Turn to Him for guidance and for strength. Invite Him into every corner of your day. Ask Him to teach you and to lead you. And remember that no matter your circumstances, God is never far away; He is here . . . always right here. So pray.

The moment you wake up each morning, all your wishes and hopes for the day rush at you like wild animals. And the first job each morning consists in shoving it all back; in listening to that other voice, taking that other point of view, letting that other, larger, stronger, quieter life come flowing in.

—

C. S. LEWIS

## MORE FROM GOD'S WORD ABOUT
## WORSHIPPING GOD EVERY DAY

*Teach me Your way, Lord, and I will live by Your truth. Give me an undivided mind to fear Your name.*

PSALM 86:11 HCSB

*I will instruct you and show you the way to go; with My eye on you, I will give counsel.*

PSALM 32:8 HCSB

*Happy is the man who finds wisdom, and the man who gains understanding.*

PROVERBS 3:13 NKJV

*But grow in the grace and knowledge of our Lord and Savior Jesus Christ. To Him be the glory both now and to the day of eternity.*

2 PETER 3:18 HCSB

*In all your ways acknowledge Him, and He shall direct your paths.*

PROVERBS 3:6 NKJV

## MORE POWERFUL IDEAS ABOUT
## YOUR DAILY DEVOTIONAL

I think that God required the Israelites to gather manna every morning so that they would learn to come to Him daily.

CYNTHIA HEALD

A person with no devotional life generally struggles with faith and obedience.

CHARLES STANLEY

Every morning God gives us the gift of comprehending anew His faithfulness of old; thus in the midst of our life with God, we may daily begin a new life with Him.

DIETRICH BONHOEFFER

Think of this—we may live together with Him here and now, a daily walking with Him who loved us and gave Himself for us.

ELISABETH ELLIOT

### A TIP FOR TODAY

Begin each day with a devotional. It is especially important during those times of your life when you're feeling discouraged, fearful, or stressed.

## A PRAYER FOR TODAY

*Dear Lord, help me to hear Your direction for my life in the solitary moments that I spend with You. And as I fulfill my responsibilities throughout the day, let my actions and my thoughts be pleasing to You. Amen*

## TODAY'S THOUGHTS

My thoughts about God's ability to transform my life and renew my strength.

_____

_____

_____

_____

_____

_____

_____

_____

_____

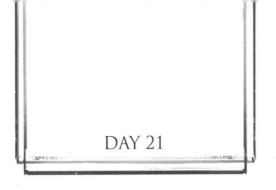

# THE RIGHT KIND OF ATTITUDE

*For God has not given us a spirit of fearfulness,
but one of power, love, and sound judgment.*

2 TIMOTHY 1:7 HCSB

Attitude is more important than the past,
than education, than money, than circumstances,
than what people do or say. It is more important than
appearance, giftedness, or skill.

—

CHARLES SWINDOLL

I f you want to build a better future for yourself and your family, you need the right kind of attitude: the positive kind. So what's your attitude today? Are you fearful, angry, bored, or worried? Are you pessimistic, perplexed, pained, and perturbed? Are you moping around with a frown on your face that's almost as big as the one in your heart? If so, God wants to have a little talk with you.

God created you in His own image, and He wants you to experience joy, contentment, peace, and abundance. But, God will not force you to experience these things; you must claim them for yourself.

God has given you free will, including the ability to influence the direction and the tone of your thoughts. And, here's how God wants you to direct those thoughts:

*Finally brothers, whatever is true, whatever is honorable, whatever is just, whatever is pure, whatever is lovely, whatever is commendable—if there is any moral excellence and if there is any praise—dwell on these things.* (Philippians 4:8 HCSB)

The quality of your attitude will help determine the quality of your life, so you must guard your thoughts accordingly. If you make up your mind to approach life with a healthy mixture of realism and optimism, you'll be rewarded. But, if you allow yourself to fall into the unfortunate habit of negative thinking, you will doom yourself to unhappiness, or mediocrity, or worse.

So, the next time you find yourself dwelling upon the negative aspects of your life, refocus your attention on things positive. The next time you find yourself falling prey to the blight of pessimism, stop yourself and turn your thoughts around. The next time you're tempted to waste valuable time gossiping or complaining, resist those temptations with all your might.

And remember: you'll never whine your way to the top . . . so don't waste your breath.

## FOLLOW HIS LEAD

God promises that He has the power to transform your life if you invite Him to do so. Your decision, then, is straightforward: whether or not to allow the Father's transforming power to work in you and through you.

God stands at the door of your heart and waits; all you must do is to invite Him in. When you do so, you cannot remain unchanged.

Is there some aspect of your life you'd like to change—a bad habit, an unhealthy relationship, or a missed opportunity? Then ask God to change your attitude and guide your path. Talk specifically to your Creator about the person you are today and the person you want to become tomorrow. When you sincerely petition the Father, you'll be amazed at the things that He and you, working together, can accomplish.

The difference between winning and losing is
how we choose to react to disappointment.

—

BARBARA JOHNSON

## MORE FROM GOD'S WORD ABOUT
## YOUR ATTITUDE

*Set your mind on things above, not on things on the earth.*

COLOSSIANS 3:2 NKJV

*Come near to God, and God will come near to you. You sinners, clean sin out of your lives. You who are trying to follow God and the world at the same time, make your thinking pure.*

JAMES 4:8 NCV

*Those who are pure in their thinking are happy, because they will be with God.*

MATTHEW 5:8 NCV

*In everything give thanks; for this is the will of God in Christ Jesus for you.*

1 THESSALONIANS 5:18 NKJV

*Worship the Lord with gladness. Come before him, singing with joy. Acknowledge that the Lord is God! He made us, and we are his. We are his people, the sheep of his pasture.*

PSALM 100:2-3 NLT

## MORE POWERFUL IDEAS ABOUT THE IMPORTANCE OF A POSITIVE ATTITUDE

The mind is like a clock that is constantly running down. It has to be wound up daily with good thoughts.

FULTON J. SHEEN

Pain is inevitable, but misery is optional.

MAX LUCADO

Your attitude is more important than your aptitude.

ZIG ZIGLAR

### A TIP FOR TODAY

A positive attitude leads to positive re-sults. If you want to improve the quality of your thoughts, ask God to help you.

We are either the masters or the victims of our attitudes. It is a matter of personal choice. Who we are today is the result of choices we made yesterday. Tomorrow, we will become what we choose today. To change means to choose to change.

JOHN MAXWELL

## A PRAYER FOR TODAY

*Lord, I pray for an attitude that is Christlike. Whatever my circumstances, whether good or bad, triumphal or tragic, let my response reflect a God-honoring attitude of optimism, faith, and love for You. Amen*

## TODAY'S THOUGHTS

My thoughts about the rewards of focusing on the positive aspects of my life, not the negative ones.

_____

_____

_____

_____

_____

_____

_____

_____

_____

_____

DAY 22

# WISDOM PROTECTS

*Acquire wisdom—how much better it is than gold!*
*And acquire understanding—*
*it is preferable to silver.*

—

PROVERBS 16:16 HCSB

If you learn from a defeat, you have not really lost.

—

ZIG ZIGLAR

Do you place a high value on the acquisition of wisdom? If so, you are not alone; most people would like to be wise, but not everyone is willing to do the work that is required to become wise. Wisdom is not like a mushroom; it does not spring up overnight. It is, instead, like an oak tree that starts as a tiny acorn, grows into a sapling, and eventually reaches up to the sky, tall and strong.

To become wise, you must seek God's guidance and live according to His Word. To become wise, you must seek instruction with consistency and purpose. To become wise, you must not only learn the lessons of the Christian life, but you must also live by them. But oftentimes, that's easier said than done.

Sometimes, amid the demands of daily life, you will lose perspective. Life may seem out of balance, and the pressures of everyday living may seem overwhelming. What's needed is a fresh perspective, a restored sense of balance . . . and God's wisdom. If you call upon the Lord and seek to see the world through His eyes, He will give you guidance, wisdom, and perspective. When you make God's priorities your priorities, He will lead you according

to His plan and according to His commandments. When you study God's teachings, you are reminded that God's reality is the ultimate reality.

Do you seek to live a life of righteousness and wisdom? If so, you must study the ultimate source of wisdom: the Word of God. You must seek out worthy mentors and listen carefully to their advice. You must associate, day in and day out, with godly men and women. Then, as you accumulate wisdom, you must not keep it for yourself; you must, instead, share it with your friends and family members.

But be forewarned: if you sincerely seek to share your hard-earned wisdom with others, your actions must reflect the values that you hold dear. The best way to share your wisdom—perhaps the only way—is not by your words, but by your example.

*So teach us to number our days,*
*that we may gain a heart of wisdom.*

—

PSALM 90:12 NKJV

## MORE FROM GOD'S WORD ABOUT HIS WISDOM

*The fear of the Lord is the beginning of wisdom; a good understanding have all those who do His commandments. His praise endures forever.*

PSALM 111:10 NKJV

*Teach me, O Lord, the way of Your statutes, and I shall keep it to the end.*

PSALM 119:33 NKJV

*A wise man will hear and increase learning, and a man of understanding will attain wise counsel.*

PROVERBS 1:5 NKJV

*Therefore, everyone who hears these words of Mine and acts on them will be like a sensible man who built his house on the rock. The rain fell, the rivers rose, and the winds blew and pounded that house. Yet it didn't collapse, because its foundation was on the rock.*

MATTHEW 7:24-25 HCSB

## MORE POWERFUL IDEAS ABOUT WISDOM

If we neglect the Bible, we cannot expect to benefit from the wisdom and direction that result from knowing God's Word.

*VONETTE BRIGHT*

When you and I are related to Jesus Christ, our strength and wisdom and peace and joy and love and hope may run out, but His life rushes in to keep us filled to the brim. We are showered with blessings, not because of anything we have or have not done, but simply because of Him.

*ANNE GRAHAM LOTZ*

Knowledge can be found in books or in school. Wisdom, on the other hand, starts with God . . . and ends there.

*MARIE T. FREEMAN*

### A TIP FOR TODAY

God makes His wisdom available to you. Your job is to acknowledge, to understand, and (above all) to use that wisdom.

This is my song through endless ages: Jesus led me all the way.

*FANNY CROSBY*

## A PRAYER FOR TODAY

*Dear Lord, when I trust in the wisdom of the world, I am often led astray, but when I trust in Your wisdom, I build my life upon a firm foundation. Today and every day I will trust Your Word and follow it, knowing that the ultimate wisdom is Your wisdom and the ultimate truth is Your truth. Amen*

## TODAY'S THOUGHTS

My thoughts about the rewards of behaving wisely and the dangers of behaving impulsively.

_____

_____

_____

_____

_____

_____

_____

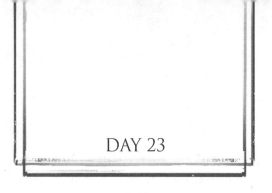

DAY 23

# YOU'RE NEVER ALONE

*The Lord is the One who will go before you.*
*He will be with you;*
*He will not leave you or forsake you.*
*Do not be afraid or discouraged.*

———

DEUTERONOMY 31:8 HCSB

It is God to whom and with whom we travel,
and while He is the End of our journey,
He is also at every stopping place.

—

ELISABETH ELLIOT

If God is everywhere, why does He sometimes seem so far away? The answer to that question, of course, has nothing to do with God and everything to do with us.

When we begin each day on our knees, in praise and worship to Him, God often seems very near indeed. But, if we ignore God's presence or—worse yet—rebel against it altogether, the world in which we live becomes a spiritual wasteland.

Are you tired, discouraged, or fearful? Be comforted because God is with you. Are you confused? Listen to the quiet voice of your Heavenly Father. Are you bitter? Talk with God and seek His guidance. Are you celebrating a great victory? Thank God and praise Him. He is the Giver of all things good.

In whatever condition you find yourself, wherever you are, whether you are happy or sad, victorious or vanquished, troubled or triumphant, celebrate God's presence. And be comforted. God is not just near. He is here.

## SPENDING QUIET MOMENTS WITH GOD

We live in an ever-changing, fast-paced world. The demands of everyday life can seem overwhelming at times, but when we slow ourselves down and seek the presence of a loving God, we invite His peace into our hearts.

Do you set aside quiet moments each day to offer praise to your Creator? You should. During these moments of stillness, you will often sense the infinite love and power of our Lord.

The familiar words of Psalm 46:10 remind us to "be still, and know that I am God" (NKJV). When we do so, we encounter the awesome presence of our loving Heavenly Father, and we are comforted in the knowledge that God is not just near. He is here.

*God did this so that men would seek him and*
*perhaps reach out for him and find him,*
*though he is not far from each one of us.*

—

ACTS 17:27 NIV

## MORE FROM GOD'S WORD ABOUT
## HIS PRESENCE

*Come near to God, and God will come near to you. You sinners, clean sin out of your lives. You who are trying to follow God and the world at the same time, make your thinking pure.*

JAMES 4:8 NCV

*No, I will not abandon you as orphans—I will come to you.*

JOHN 14:18 NLT

*Again, this is God's command: to believe in his personally named Son, Jesus Christ. He told us to love each other, in line with the original command. As we keep his commands, we live deeply and surely in him, and he lives in us. And this is how we experience his deep and abiding presence in us: by the Spirit he gave us.*

1 JOHN 3:23-24 MSG

*For the eyes of the Lord range throughout the earth to strengthen those whose hearts are fully committed to him.*

2 CHRONICLES 16:9 NIV

## MORE POWERFUL IDEAS ABOUT GOD'S PRESENCE

God is every moment totally aware of each one of us. Totally aware in intense concentration and love. No one passes through any area of life, happy or tragic, without the attention of God with Him.

EUGENIA PRICE

We should learn to live in the presence of the living God. He should be a well for us: delightful, comforting, unfailing, springing up to eternal life (John 4:14). When we rely on other people, their water supplies ultimately dry up. But, the well of the Creator never fails to nourish us.

C. H. SPURGEON

### A TIP FOR TODAY

Slow yourself down, tune out the distractions, and listen. God has important things to say; your task is to be still and listen.

Get yourself into the presence of the loving Father. Just place yourself before Him, and look up into, His face; think of His love, His wonderful, tender, pitying love.

ANDREW MURRAY

## A PRAYER FOR TODAY

*Heavenly Father, even when it seems to me that You are far away, You never leave my side. Today and every day, I will strive to feel Your presence, and I will strive to sense Your love for me. Amen*

## TODAY'S THOUGHTS

My thoughts about the importance of finding quiet time each day to sense God's presence and His love.

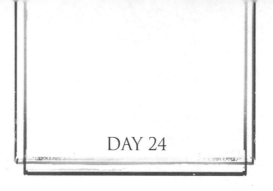

DAY 24

# EMBRACING CHANGE

*His message was simple and austere,*
*like his desert surroundings: "Change your life.*
*God's kingdom is here."*

—

MATTHEW 3:2 MSG

Resistance to change is universal.
It invades all classes and cultures.
There is nothing more difficult to undertake or
more uncertain in its success,
than introducing change.

—

JOHN MAXWELL

I n our fast-paced world, everyday life has become an ex-
ercise in managing change. Our circumstances change;
our relationships change; our bodies change. We grow
older every day, as does our world. Thankfully, God does
not change. He is eternal, as are the truths that are found
in His Holy Word.

The ideas in this book are intended to help you accept
change—and embrace it—as you continue to seek God's
unfolding plan for your life.

Are you a woman who is facing one of life's inevitable
"mid-course corrections"? If so, you must place your faith,
your trust, and your life in the hands of the One who does
not change: your Heavenly Father. He is the unmoving
rock upon which you must construct this day and every
day. When you do, you are secure.

## ANTICIPATING YOUR NEXT GRAND ADVENTURE

It has been said that a rut is nothing more than a grave with both ends kicked out. That's a thought worth pondering. Have you made your life an exciting adventure, or have you allowed the distractions of everyday life to rob you of a sense of God's purpose?

As a believing Christian, you have every reason to celebrate. So if you find yourself feeling as if you're stuck in a rut, or in an unfortunate circumstance, or in a difficult relationship, abandon the status quo by making the changes that your heart tells you are right. After all, in God's glorious kingdom, there should be no place for disciples who are dejected, discouraged, or disheartened. God has a far better plan than that, and so should you.

> With God, it isn't who you were that matters;
> it's who you are becoming.
>
> —
>
> LIZ CURTIS HIGGS

## MORE FROM GOD'S WORD ABOUT TRUST

*Trust in the Lord with all your heart, and do not rely on your own understanding; think about Him in all your ways, and He will guide you on the right paths.*

PROVERBS 3:5-6 HCSB

*Let us hold fast the confession of our hope without wavering, for He who promised is faithful.*

HEBREWS 10:23 NKJV

*For we walk by faith, not by sight.*

2 CORINTHIANS 5:7 NKJV

*The one who understands a matter finds success, and the one who trusts in the Lord will be happy.*

PROVERBS 16:20 HCSB

*For the eyes of the Lord range throughout the earth to show Himself strong for those whose hearts are completely His.*

2 CHRONICLES 16:9 HCSB

## MORE POWERFUL IDEAS ABOUT CHANGE

More often than not, when something looks like it's the absolute end, it is really the beginning.

CHARLES SWINDOLL

In a world kept chaotic by change, you will eventually discover, as I have, that this is one of the most precious qualities of the God we are looking for: He doesn't change.

BILL HYBELS

Mere change is not growth. Growth is the synthesis of change and continuity, and where there is no continuity there is no growth.

C. S. LEWIS

### A TIP FOR TODAY

Change is inevitable. Do not fear it. Embrace it.

The secret of contentment in the midst of change is found in having roots in the changeless Christ—the same yesterday, today and forever.

ED YOUNG

## A PRAYER FOR TODAY

*Dear Lord, our world is constantly changing. When I face the inevitable transitions of life, I will turn to You for strength and assurance. Thank You, Father, for love that is unchanging and everlasting. Amen*

## TODAY'S THOUGHTS

My thoughts about the need to embrace the changes that God has placed along my path.

_____

_____

_____

_____

_____

_____

_____

_____

_____

# TOO FOCUSED ON POSSESSIONS?

*Don't collect for yourselves treasures on earth, where moth and rust destroy and where thieves break in and steal. But collect for yourselves treasures in heaven, where neither moth nor rust destroys, and where thieves don't break in and steal. For where your treasure is, there your heart will be also.*

—

MATTHEW 6:19-21 HCSB

It's sobering to contemplate how much time, effort, sacrifice, compromise, and attention we give to acquiring and increasing our supply of something that is totally insignificant in eternity.

—

ANNE GRAHAM LOTZ

All too often we focus our thoughts and energies on the accumulation of earthly treasures, creating untold stress in our lives and leaving precious little time to accumulate the only treasures that really matter: the spiritual kind. Our material possessions have the potential to do great good—depending upon how we use them. If we allow the things we own to own us, we may pay dearly for our misplaced priorities.

Society focuses intently on material possessions, but God's Word teaches us time and again that money matters little when compared to the spiritual gifts that the Creator offers to those who put Him first in their lives. So today, keep your possessions in perspective. Remember that God should come first, and everything else next. When you give God His rightful place in your heart, you'll have a clearer vision of the things that really matter. Then, you can joyfully thank your Heavenly Father for spiritual blessings that are, in truth, too numerous to count.

## OUR REAL RICHES

How important are your material possessions? Not as important as you might think. In the life of a committed Christian, material possessions should play a rather small role. In fact, when we become overly enamored with the things we own, we needlessly distance ourselves from the peace that God offers to those who place Him at the center of their lives.

Of course, we all need the basic necessities of life, but once we meet those needs for ourselves and for our families, the piling up of possessions creates more problems than it solves. Our real riches, of course, are not of this world. We are never really rich until we are rich in spirit.

Do you find yourself wrapped up in the concerns of the material world? If so, it's time to reorder your priorities by turning your thoughts and your prayers to more important matters. And, it's time to begin storing up riches that will endure throughout eternity: the spiritual kind.

We are made spiritually lethargic by
a steady diet of materialism.

—

MARY MORRISON SUGGS

## MORE FROM GOD'S WORD ABOUT MATERIALISM

*Do not love the world or the things in the world. If anyone loves the world, the love of the Father is not in him.*

1 JOHN 2:15 NKJV

*He who trusts in his riches will fall, but the righteous will flourish.*

PROVERBS 11:28 NKJV

*For what will it profit a man if he gains the whole world, and loses his own soul? Or what will a man give in exchange for his soul?*

MARK 8:36-37 NKJV

*For where your treasure is, there your heart will be also.*

LUKE 12:34 NKJV

*Since we entered the world penniless and will leave it penniless, if we have bread on the table and shoes on our feet, that's enough.*

1 TIMOTHY 6:7-8 MSG

## MORE POWERFUL IDEAS ABOUT MATERIALISM

Greed is enslaving. The more you have, the more you want—until eventually avarice consumes you.

KAY ARTHUR

A society that pursues pleasure runs the risk of raising expectations ever higher, so that true contentment always lies tantalizingly out of reach.

PHILIP YANCEY AND PAUL BRAND

Outside appearances, things like the clothes you wear or the car you drive, are important to other people but totally unimportant to God. Trust God.

MARIE T. FREEMAN

### A TIP FOR TODAY

Genuine happiness comes not from money, but from the things that money can't buy— starting with your relationship to God.

Here's a simple test: If you can see it, it's not going to last. The things that last are the things you cannot see.

DENNIS SWANBERG

164

## A PRAYER FOR TODAY

*Heavenly Father, when I focus intently upon You, I am blessed. When I focus too intently on material possessions, I am troubled. Make my priorities pleasing to You, Father, and make me a worthy servant of Your Son. Amen*

## TODAY'S THOUGHTS

My thoughts about the dangers of materialism.

_____

_____

_____

_____

_____

_____

_____

_____

_____

_____

DAY 26

# FINDING STRENGTH
# AND SECURITY

*I can do all things through Christ
who strengthens me.*

—

PHILIPPIANS 4:13 NKJV

When trials come your way—as inevitably they will—
do not run away.
Run to your God and Father.

—

KAY ARTHUR

God's love and support never changes. From the cradle to the grave, God has promised to give you the strength to meet any challenge. God has promised to lift you up and guide your steps if you let Him. God has promised that when you entrust your life to Him completely and without reservation, He will give you the courage to face any trial, the wisdom to live in His righteousness, and the everlasting security of His love.

God's hand uplifts those who turn their hearts and prayers to Him. Will you count yourself among that number? Will you accept God's peace and wear God's armor against the temptations and distractions of our dangerous world? If you do, you can live courageously and optimistically, knowing that you have been forever touched by the loving, unfailing, uplifting hand of God.

## HE IS SUFFICIENT

Of this you can be certain: God is sufficient to meet your needs. Period.

Do the demands of life seem overwhelming at times? If so, you must learn to rely not only upon your own resources, but also upon the promises of your Father in heaven. God will hold your hand and walk with you and your family if you let Him. So even if your circumstances are difficult, trust the Father.

God promises that He is "near to those who have a broken heart" (Psalm 34:18 NKJV). When we are troubled, we must turn to Him, and we must encourage our friends and family members to do likewise.

If you are discouraged by the inevitable demands of life here on earth, be mindful of this fact: the loving heart of God is sufficient to meet any challenge . . . including yours.

A divine strength is given to those who yield themselves
to the Father and obey what He tells them to do.

—

WARREN WIERSBE

## MORE FROM GOD'S WORD ABOUT
## FINDING STRENGTH

*Be strong! We must prove ourselves strong for our people and for the cities of our God. May the Lord's will be done.*

1 CHRONICLES 19:13 HCSB

*And He said to me, "My grace is sufficient for you, for My strength is made perfect in weakness."*

2 CORINTHIANS 12:9 NKJV

*Finally, be strengthened by the Lord and by His vast strength.*

EPHESIANS 6:10 HCSB

*The LORD is my strength and my song.*

EXODUS 15:2 NIV

*Those who hope in the LORD will renew their strength. They will soar on wings like eagles; they will run and not grow weary, they will walk and not be faint.*

ISAIAH 40:31 NIV

## MORE POWERFUL IDEAS ABOUT
## FINDING STRENGTH

The same God who empowered Samson, Gideon, and Paul seeks to empower my life and your life, because God hasn't changed.

BILL HYBELS

A divine strength is given to those who yield themselves to the Father and obey what He tells them to do.

WARREN WIERSBE

If we take God's program, we can have God's power—not otherwise.

E. STANLEY JONES

### A TIP FOR TODAY

If you're tempted to give up on yourself, remember that God will never give up on you. And when God is in your corner, you have nothing to fear.

No matter how heavy the burden, daily strength is given, so I expect we need not give ourselves any concern as to what the outcome will be. We must simply go forward.

ANNIE ARMSTRONG

## A PRAYER FOR TODAY

*Lord, sometimes life is difficult. Sometimes, I am worried, weary, or heartbroken. But, when I lift my eyes to You, Father, You strengthen me. When I am weak, You lift me up. Today, I turn to You, Lord, for my strength, for my hope, and for my salvation. Amen*

## TODAY'S THOUGHTS

My thoughts about finding strength through God's promises.

_____

_____

_____

_____

_____

_____

_____

_____

_____

DAY 27

# IN TOUGH TIMES, GOD TEACHES AND LEADS

*Leave inexperience behind, and you will live;*
*pursue the way of understanding.*

—

PROVERBS 9:6 HCSB

Your greatest ministry will likely
come out of your greatest hurt.

—

RICK WARREN

When it comes to your faith, God doesn't intend for you to stand still. He wants you to keep moving and growing. In fact, God's plan for you includes a lifetime of prayer, praise, and spiritual growth.

When we cease to grow, either emotionally or spiritually, we do ourselves and our loved ones a profound disservice. But, if we study God's Word, if we obey His commandments, and if we live in the center of His will, we will not be "stagnant" believers; we will, instead, be growing Christians . . . and that's exactly what God wants for our lives.

Many of life's most important lessons are painful to learn. During times of heartbreak and hardship, we must be courageous and we must be patient, knowing that in His own time, God will heal us if we invite Him into our hearts.

Spiritual growth need not take place only in times of adversity. We must seek to grow in our knowledge and love of the Lord every day that we live. In those quiet moments when we open our hearts to God, the One who made us

keeps remaking us. He gives us direction, perspective, wisdom, and courage. The appropriate moment to accept those spiritual gifts is the present one.

Are you as mature as you're ever going to be? Hopefully not! When it comes to your faith, God doesn't intend for you to become "fully grown," at least not in this lifetime. In fact, God still has important lessons that He intends to teach you. So ask yourself this: What lesson is God trying to teach me today? And then go about the business of learning it.

## WHERE IS GOD LEADING?

Whether we realize it or not, times of adversity can be times of intense personal and spiritual growth. Our difficult days are also times when we can learn and relearn some of life's most important lessons.

The next time you experience a difficult moment, a difficult day, or a difficult year, ask yourself this question: Where is God leading me? In times of struggle and sorrow, you can be certain that God is leading you to a place of His choosing. Your duty is to watch, to pray, to listen, and to follow.

## MORE FROM GOD'S WORD ABOUT
## SPIRITUAL GROWTH

*For this reason we also, since the day we heard it, do not cease to pray for you, and to ask that you may be filled with the knowledge of His will in all wisdom and spiritual understanding.*

COLOSSIANS 1:9 NKJV

*So let us stop going over the basics of Christianity again and again. Let us go on instead and become mature in our understanding.*

HEBREWS 6:1 NLT

*Run away from infantile indulgence. Run after mature righteousness—faith, love, peace—joining those who are in honest and serious prayer before God.*

2 TIMOTHY 2:22 MSG

*For You, O God, have tested us; You have refined us as silver is refined. You brought us into the net; You laid affliction on our backs. You have caused men to ride over our heads; we went through fire and through water; but You brought us out to rich fulfillment.*

PSALM 66:10-12 NKJV

## MORE POWERFUL IDEAS ABOUT
## SPIRITUAL GROWTH

Let's thank God for allowing us to experience troubles that drive us closer to Him.

SHIRLEY DOBSON

Comfort and prosperity have never enriched the world as much as adversity has.

BILLY GRAHAM

Meditation is as silver; but tribulation is as fine gold.

C. H. SPURGEON

### A TIP FOR TODAY

Times of change can be times of growth and can lead to a renewal of spirit.

Growth in depth and strength and consistency and fruitfulness and ultimately in Christlikeness is only possible when the winds of life are contrary to personal comfort.

ANNE GRAHAM LOTZ

## A PRAYER FOR TODAY

*Dear Lord, when I open myself to You, I am blessed. Let me accept Your love and Your wisdom, Father. Show me Your way, and deliver me from the painful mistakes that I make when I stray from Your commandments. Let me live according to Your Word, and let me grow in my faith every day that I live. Amen*

## TODAY'S THOUGHTS

My thoughts about the rewards of growing emotionally and spiritually.

_____

_____

_____

_____

_____

_____

_____

_____

DAY 28

# BE THANKFUL AND WORSHIP HIM

*Therefore as you have received Christ Jesus*
*the Lord, walk in Him, rooted and built up in Him*
*and established in the faith, just as you were taught,*
*and overflowing with thankfulness.*

COLOSSIANS 2:6-7 HCSB

God has promised that if we harvest well
with the tools of thanksgiving, there will be seeds for
planting in the spring.

*GLORIA GAITHER*

As believing Christians, we are blessed beyond measure. God sent His only Son to die for our sins. And, God has given us the priceless gifts of eternal love and eternal life. We, in turn, are instructed to approach our Heavenly Father with reverence and thanksgiving. But sometimes, in the crush of everyday living, we simply don't stop long enough to pause and thank our Creator for the countless blessings He has bestowed upon us.

When we slow down and express our gratitude to the One who made us, we enrich our own lives and the lives of those around us. Thanksgiving should become a habit, a regular part of our daily routines. God has blessed us beyond measure, and we owe Him everything, including our eternal praise.

Are you a thankful person? Do you appreciate the gifts that God has given you? And, do you demonstrate your gratitude by being a faithful steward of the gifts and talents that you have received from your Creator? You most certainly should be thankful. After all, when you stop to think about it, God has given you more blessings than you

can count. So the question of the day is this: Will you thank your Heavenly Father . . . or will you spend your time and energy doing other things?

God is always listening—are you willing to say thanks? It's up to you, and the next move is yours.

## WORSHIP HIM TODAY

God has a wonderful plan for your life, and an important part of that plan includes worship. We should never deceive ourselves: every life is based upon some form of worship. The question is not whether we worship, but what we worship.

Some of us choose to worship God. The result is a plentiful harvest of joy, peace, and abundance. Others distance themselves from God by foolishly worshiping earthly possessions and personal gratification. To do so is a mistake of profound proportions.

Have you accepted the grace of God's only begotten Son? Then worship Him. Worship Him today and every day. Worship Him with sincerity and thanksgiving. Write His name on your heart and rest assured that He, too, has written your name on His.

## MORE FROM GOD'S WORD ABOUT
## THANKSGIVING

*Thanks be to God for His indescribable gift.*

2 CORINTHIANS 9:15 HCSB

*And let the peace of the Messiah, to which you were also called in one body, control your hearts. Be thankful.*

COLOSSIANS 3:15 HCSB

*It is good to give thanks to the Lord, and to sing praises to Your name, O Most High.*

PSALM 92:1 NKJV

*Praise the Lord! Oh, give thanks to the Lord, for He is good! For His mercy endures forever.*

PSALM 106:1 NKJV

*In everything give thanks; for this is the will of God in Christ Jesus for you.*

2 THESSALONIANS 5:18 NKJV

## MORE POWERFUL IDEAS ABOUT
## THANKSGIVING

It is always possible to be thankful for what is given rather than to complain about what is not given. One or the other becomes a habit of life.

ELISABETH ELLIOT

Thanksgiving or complaining—these words express two contrastive attitudes of the souls of God's children in regard to His dealings with them. The soul that gives thanks can find comfort in everything; the soul that complains can find comfort in nothing.

HANNAH WHITALL SMITH

### A TIP FOR TODAY

You owe God everything . . . including your thanks.

Praise and thank God for who He is and for what He has done for you.

BILLY GRAHAM

Spiritual worship is focusing all we are on all He is.

BETH MOORE

## A PRAYER FOR TODAY

*Heavenly Father, let today and every day be a time of worship. Let me worship You, not only with words and deeds, but also with my heart. In the quiet moments of the day, let me praise You and thank You for creating me, loving me, guiding me, and saving me. Amen*

## TODAY'S THOUGHTS

My thoughts about the many ways God has blessed me and my loved ones.

_____

_____

_____

_____

_____

_____

_____

_____

# YOUR VERY BRIGHT FUTURE

*For I know the thoughts that I think toward you,*
*says the Lord, thoughts of peace and not of evil,*
*to give you a future and a hope. Then you will call*
*upon Me and go and pray to Me,*
*and I will listen to you.*

—

JEREMIAH 29:11-12 NKJV

Our future may look fearfully intimidating,
yet we can look up to the Engineer of the Universe,
confident that nothing escapes His attention or slips out
of the control of those strong hands.

—

ELISABETH ELLIOT

Because we are saved by a risen Christ, we can have hope for the future, no matter how troublesome our present circumstances may seem. After all, God has promised that we are His throughout eternity. And, He has told us that we must place our hopes in Him.

Of course, we will face disappointments and failures while we are here on earth, but these are only temporary defeats. This world can be a place of trials and tribulations, but when we place our trust in the Giver of all things good, we are secure. God has promised us peace, joy, and eternal life. And God keeps His promises today, tomorrow, and forever.

Are you willing to place your future in the hands of a loving and all-knowing God? Do you trust in the ultimate goodness of His plan for your life? Will you face today's challenges with optimism and hope? You should. After all, God created you for a very important purpose: His purpose. And you still have important work to do: His work.

Today, as you live in the present and look to the future, remember that God has a plan for you. Act—and believe—accordingly.

## LET GOD BE YOUR GUIDE

The Bible promises that God will guide you if you let Him. Your job, of course, is to let Him. But sometimes, you will be tempted to do otherwise. Sometimes, you'll be tempted to go along with the crowd; other times, you'll be tempted to do things your way, not God's way. When you feel those temptations, you must resist them, or else.

What will you allow to guide you through the coming day: your own desires (or, for that matter, the desires of your peers)? Or will you allow God to lead the way? The answer should be obvious. You should let God be your guide. When you entrust your life to Him completely and without reservation, God will give you the strength to meet any challenge, the courage to face any trial, and the wisdom to live in His righteousness. So trust Him today and seek His guidance. When you do, your character will most certainly take care of itself, and your next step will most assuredly be the right one.

## MORE FROM GOD'S WORD ABOUT
## HIS GUIDANCE

*In all your ways acknowledge Him, and He shall direct your paths.*

PROVERBS 3:6 NKJV

*For now we see indistinctly, as in a mirror, but then face to face. Now I know in part, but then I will know fully, as I am fully known.*

1 CORINTHIANS 13:12 HCSB

*However, each one must live his life in the situation the Lord assigned when God called him.*

1 CORINTHIANS 7:17 HCSB

*The earth and everything in it, the world and its inhabitants, belong to the Lord.*

PSALM 24:1 HCSB

*My cup runs over. Surely goodness and mercy shall follow me all the days of my life; and I will dwell in the house of the Lord forever.*

PSALM 23:5-6 NKJV

## MORE POWERFUL IDEAS ABOUT YOUR FUTURE

The future lies all before us. Shall it only be a slight advance upon what we usually do? Ought it not to be a bound, a leap forward to altitudes of endeavor and success undreamed of before?

ANNIE ARMSTRONG

Every experience God gives us, every person he brings into our lives, is the perfect preparation for the future that only he can see.

CORRIE TEN BOOM

The Christian believes in a fabulous future.

BILLY GRAHAM

### A TIP FOR TODAY

God will guide you if you let Him. You job is to acknowledge Him and to follow closely in the footsteps of His Son.

Are you serious about wanting God's guidance to become a personal reality in your life? The first step is to tell God that you know you can't manage your own life; that you need his help.

CATHERINE MARSHALL

188

## A PRAYER FOR TODAY

*Dear Lord, as I look to the future, I will place my trust in You. If I become discouraged, I will turn to You. If I am afraid, I will seek strength in You. You are my Father, and I will place my hope, my trust, and my faith in You. Amen*

## TODAY'S THOUGHTS

My thoughts about the bright future—and the eternal life—that is mine through Christ.

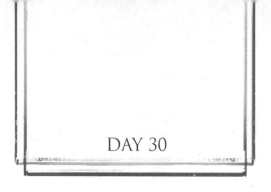

DAY 30

# FOLLOW HIM

*Then Jesus said to His disciples,*
*"If anyone wants to come with Me, he must deny*
*himself, take up his cross, and follow Me.*
*For whoever wants to save his life will lose it,*
*but whoever loses his life because of Me will find it."*

—

MATTHEW 16:24-25 HCSB

The Christian faith is meant to be lived
moment by moment. It isn't some broad,
general outline—it's a long walk with a real Person.
Details count: passing thoughts, small sacrifices,
a few encouraging words, little acts of kindness,
brief victories over nagging sins.

JONI EARECKSON TADA

Jesus walks with you. Are you walking with Him seven days a week, and not just on Sunday mornings? Are you a seven-day-a-week Christian who carries your faith with you to work each day, or do you try to keep Jesus at a "safe" distance when you're not sitting in church? Hopefully, you understand the wisdom of walking with Christ all day every day.

Jesus loved you so much that He endured unspeakable humiliation and suffering for you. How will you respond to Christ's sacrifice? Will you take up His cross and follow Him—during good times and tough times—or will you choose another path? When you place your hopes squarely at the foot of the cross, when you place Jesus squarely at the center of your life, you will be blessed.

Do you seek to fulfill God's purpose for your life? Do you seek spiritual abundance? Would you like to partake in "the peace that passes all understanding"? Then fol-

low Christ. Follow Him by picking up His cross today and every day that you live. When you do, you will quickly discover that Christ's love has the power to change everything, including you.

## YOUR ETERNAL JOURNEY

Eternal life is not an event that begins when you die. Eternal life begins when you invite Jesus into your heart right here on earth. So it's important to remember that God's plans for you are not limited to the ups and downs of everyday life. If you've allowed Jesus to reign over your heart, you've already begun your eternal journey.

Today, give praise to the Creator for His priceless gift, the gift of eternal life. And then, when you've offered Him your thanks and your praise, share His Good News with all who cross your path.

## MORE FROM GOD'S WORD ABOUT
## FOLLOWING CHRIST

*Then he told them what they could expect for themselves:
"Anyone who intends to come with me has to let me lead."*

LUKE 9:23 MSG

*I've laid down a pattern for you. What I've done, you do.*

JOHN 13:15 MSG

*No one can serve two masters. Either he will hate the one and
love the other, or he will be devoted to the one and despise the
other.*

MATTHEW 6:24 NIV

*Whoever is not willing to carry the cross and follow me is not
worthy of me. Those who try to hold on to their lives will give
up true life. Those who give up their lives for me will hold on
to true life.*

MATTHEW 10:38-39 NCV

*If anyone would come after me, he must deny himself and take
up his cross and follow me.*

MARK 8:34 NIV

## MORE POWERFUL IDEAS ABOUT FOLLOWING CHRIST

Jesus Christ is not a security from storms. He is perfect security in storms.

KATHY TROCCOLI

I can tell you, from personal experience of walking with God for over fifty years, that He is the Lover of my soul.

VONETTE BRIGHT

The Lord gets His best soldiers out of the highlands of affliction.

C. H. SPURGEON

## A TIP FOR TODAY

If you want to be a little more like Jesus, learn about His teachings, follow in His footsteps, and obey His commandments.

In the midst of the pressure and the heat, I am confident His hand is on my life, developing my faith until I display His glory, transforming me into a vessel of honor that pleases Him!

ANNE GRAHAM LOTZ

## A PRAYER FOR TODAY

*Dear Jesus, because I am Your disciple, I will trust You, I will obey Your teachings, and I will share Your Good News. You have given me life abundant and life eternal, and I will follow You today and forever. Amen*

## TODAY'S THOUGHTS

My thoughts about the genuine joys and eternal rewards of following Jesus.

_____

_____

_____

_____

_____

_____

_____

_____

There is no safer place to live
than the center of His will.

—

CALVIN MILLER

# APPENDIX

# MORE FROM GOD'S WORD

## LOVE

*No one has greater love than this, that someone would lay down his life for his friends.*

JOHN 15:13 HCSB

*Dear friends, if God loved us in this way, we also must love one another.*

1 JOHN 4:11 HCSB

*Love one another earnestly from a pure heart.*

1 PETER 1:22 HCSB

*Above all, keep your love for one another at full strength, since love covers a multitude of sins.*

1 PETER 4:8 HCSB

*And may the Lord cause you to increase and overflow with love for one another and for everyone, just as we also do for you.*

1 THESSALONIANS 3:12 HCSB

## SILENCE

*Happy is the man who finds wisdom, and the man who gains understanding.*

PROVERBS 3:13 NKJV

*I sought the Lord, and He heard me, and delivered me from all my fears.*

PSALM 34:4 NKJV

### *Be still, and know that I am God.*

PSALM 46:10 NKJV

*Be silent before the Lord and wait expectantly for Him.*

PSALM 37:7 HCSB

*In quietness and confidence shall be your strength.*

ISAIAH 30:15 NKJV

*I am not alone, because the Father is with Me.*

JOHN 16:32 HCSB

## LEADERSHIP

*For an overseer, as God's manager, must be blameless, not arrogant, not quick tempered, not addicted to wine, not a bully, not greedy for money.*

TITUS 1:7 HCSB

*According to the grace given to us, we have different gifts: If prophecy, use it according to the standard of faith; if service, in service; if teaching, in teaching; if exhorting, in exhortation; giving, with generosity; leading, with diligence; showing mercy, with cheerfulness.*

ROMANS 12:6-8 HCSB

*Shepherd God's flock among you, not overseeing out of compulsion but freely, according to God's will; not for the money but eagerly.*

1 PETER 5:2 HCSB

*And we exhort you, brothers: warn those who are lazy, comfort the discouraged, help the weak, be patient with everyone.*

1 THESSALONIANS 5:14 HCSB

## ABUNDANCE

*I have come that they may have life, and that they may have it more abundantly.*

JOHN 10:10 NKJV

*And God is able to make every grace overflow to you, so that in every way, always having everything you need, you may excel in every good work.*

2 CORINTHIANS 9:8 HCSB

*Until now you have asked for nothing in My name. Ask and you will receive, that your joy may be complete.*

JOHN 16:24 HCSB

*Come to terms with God and be at peace;*
*in this way good will come to you.*

JOB 22:21 HCSB

*My cup runs over. Surely goodness and mercy shall follow me all the days of my life; and I will dwell in the house of the Lord forever.*

PSALM 23:5-6 NKJV

## MATURITY

*A wise man will hear, and will increase learning;*
*and a man of understanding shall attain*
*unto wise counsels....*

PROVERBS 1:5 KJV

Do not be conformed to this age, but be transformed by the renewing of your mind, so that you may discern what is the good, pleasing, and perfect will of God.

ROMANS 12:2 HCSB

When I was a child, I spoke like a child, I thought like a child, I reasoned like a child. When I became a man, I put aside childish things.

1 CORINTHIANS 13:11 HCSB

Consider it a great joy, my brothers, whenever you experience various trials, knowing that the testing of your faith produces endurance. But endurance must do its complete work, so that you may be mature and complete, lacking nothing.

JAMES 1:2-4 HCSB

## DISCIPLESHIP

*Anyone who listens to me is happy, watching at my doors every day, waiting by the posts of my doorway. For the one who finds me finds life and obtains favor from the Lord, but the one who sins against me harms himself; all who hate me love death.*

PROVERBS 8:34-36 HCSB

*He has told you men what is good and what it is the Lord requires of you: Only to act justly, to love faithfulness, and to walk humbly with your God.*

MICAH 6:8 HCSB

*Therefore, be imitators of God,
as dearly loved children.*

EPHESIANS 5:1 HCSB

*We always pray for you that our God will consider you worthy of His calling, and will, by His power, fulfill every desire for goodness and the work of faith, so that the name of our Lord Jesus will be glorified by you, and you by Him, according to the grace of our God and the Lord Jesus Christ.*

2 THESSALONIANS 1:11-12 HCSB

## EXAMPLE

*Love and truth form a good leader;*
*sound leadership is founded on loving integrity.*

PROVERBS 20:28 MSG

*You should be an example to the believers in speech, in conduct,*
*in love, in faith, in purity.*

1 TIMOTHY 4:12 HCSB

*Therefore since we also have such a large cloud of witnesses*
*surrounding us, let us lay aside every weight and the sin that*
*so easily ensnares us, and run with endurance the race that lies*
*before us.*

HEBREWS 12:1 HCSB

*Set an example of good works yourself, with integrity and*
*dignity in your teaching.*

TITUS 2:7 HCSB

*Do everything without grumbling and arguing, so that you may*
*be blameless and pure.*

PHILIPPIANS 2:14-15 HCSB

## ANGER

*Everyone must be quick to hear, slow to speak, and slow to anger, for man's anger does not accomplish God's righteousness.*

JAMES 1:19-20 HCSB

*A patient person [shows] great understanding, but a quick-tempered one promotes foolishness.*

PROVERBS 14:29 HCSB

*But now you must also put away all the following: anger, wrath, malice, slander, and filthy language from your mouth.*

COLOSSIANS 3:8 HCSB

*Don't let your spirit rush to be angry, for anger abides in the heart of fools.*

ECCLESIASTES 7:9 HCSB

*All bitterness, anger and wrath, insult and slander must be removed from you, along with all wickedness. And be kind and compassionate to one another, forgiving one another, just as God also forgave you in Christ.*

EPHESIANS 4:31-32 HCSB

## GENEROSITY

*The generous soul will be made rich, and he who waters will also be watered himself.*

*Freely you have received, freely give.*

PROVERBS 11:25 NKJV

MATTHEW 10:8 NKJV

*As each one has received a gift, minister it to one another, as good stewards of the manifold grace of God.*

1 PETER 4:10 NKJV

*But this I say: He who sows sparingly will also reap sparingly, and he who sows bountifully will also reap bountifully. So let each one give as he purposes in his heart, not grudgingly or of necessity; for God loves a cheerful giver.*

2 CORINTHIANS 9:6-7 NKJV

*Cast your bread upon the waters, For you will find it after many days.*

ECCLESIASTES 11:1 NKJV

## DREAMS

*Now may the God of hope fill you with all joy and peace in believing, so that you may overflow with hope by the power of the Holy Spirit.*

ROMANS 15:13 HCSB

*Where there is no vision, the people perish.*

PROVERBS 29:18 KJV

*Be of good courage, and he shall strengthen your heart, all ye that hope in the LORD.*

PSALM 31:24 KJV

*Therefore, as we have opportunity, we must work for the good of all, especially for those who belong to the household of faith.*

GALATIANS 6:10 HCSB

*But as it is written: What no eye has seen and no ear has heard, and what has never come into a man's heart, is what God has prepared for those who love Him.*

1 CORINTHIANS 2:9 HCSB

## ENCOURAGING OTHERS

*I want their hearts to be encouraged and joined together in love, so that they may have all the riches of assured understanding, and have the knowledge of God's mystery—Christ.*

COLOSSIANS 2:2 HCSB

*And let us be concerned about one another in order to promote love and good works.*

HEBREWS 10:24 HCSB

*Carry one another's burdens; in this way you will fulfill the law of Christ.*

GALATIANS 6:2 HCSB

*But encourage each other daily, while it is still called today, so that none of you is hardened by sin's deception.*

HEBREWS 3:13 HCSB

*Anxiety in a man's heart weighs it down, but a good word cheers it up.*

PROVERBS 12:25 HCSB